OPPORTUNITIES

in

P9-CSC-774

Child Care Careers

REVISED EDITION

RENEE WITTENBERG

Mc
Graw
Hill

New York Chicago San Francisco Lisbon London Madrid Mexico City
Milan New Delhi San Juan Seoul Singapore Sydney Toronto

Library of Congress Cataloging-in-Publication Data

Wittenberg, Renee.
    Opportunities in child care careers / by Renee Wittenberg. — Rev. ed.
       p.   cm.
    Includes bibliographical references.
    ISBN 0-07-146766-1 (alk. paper)
    1. Child care—Vocational guidance—United States.   I. Title.

  HQ778.7.U6W57   2007
  362.71'202373—dc22   2006001324

1 2 3 4 5 6 7 8 9 10 11 12 13 14 15 16 17 18 19   DOC/DOC   0 9 8 7 6

ISBN-13: 978-0-07-146766-7
ISBN-10:   0-07-146766-1

Interior design by Rattray Design

McGraw-Hill books are available at special quantity discounts to use as premiums and sales promotions, or for use in corporate training programs. For more information, please write to the Director of Special Sales, Professional Publishing, McGraw-Hill, Two Penn Plaza, New York, NY 10121-2298. Or contact your local bookstore.

This book is printed on acid-free paper.

CONTENTS

iii

programs. States given block grants. The Handicapped
Act. Smart Start. The 1990 child care bill. The
beginning of a new perspective. No Child Left Behind
Act. Good Start, Grow Smart Early Childhood
Initiative. Conclusion.

takeover. Unions and labor laws. Job outlook. Need
for supporting child care. Child care earnings.

Foreword

THERE ARE MANY types of careers available in this field that will appeal to whatever an individual may be looking for. Some seek adventure. Some seek travel. Some seek fame or money. Then there are those who seek the fulfillment of shaping the future of a nation. Whatever the motivating force may be, those who choose careers in child care are said to fulfill an essential societal role.

Never thought of it in that manner? Societal shaping can be accomplished by working in a form of public service, for example, in public office or some other form of government service. It can also be accomplished by working one on one with the people who will operate our country in the future—children.

Working in child care can be challenging and fulfilling. The knowledge that what you do today may affect a child for the rest of his or her life is a heavy responsibility. I have met many fine caregivers during the years I worked in and around child care. They all take their responsibility seriously, and they truly enjoy their work with children.

Teaching children to do their best and to be successful in life does not begin when they start school. It begins at birth. Humans form their basic personalities from the first few weeks through the first few years. By the time children reach school, basic traits, eating habits, and a sense of self are already well established.

Our society has evolved from one in which children are taken care of in an extended family or village atmosphere to a society in which children are increasingly cared for in a child care setting.

Our extended families are often scattered all over the country or even around the world. The once-small community is now a city of thousands or millions. Our mobility as a society is ever increasing. What grandparents, aunts and uncles, brothers and sisters, and neighbors once did is gone for the majority of us. The family support system has changed.

In many cases, the child care professional actually spends more waking hours with young children than the parents do. They have an active role in shaping the children's self-esteem, education, healthy habits, social skills, and nutritional patterns.

We are all products of our early environment. It is our society's obligation to ensure we provide the best environment for our children. Failure to do so will be an expensive price to pay.

The individuals who work on a day-to-day basis with our children are key to our success as a society.

I would encourage those who are serious about the well-being of our children and, even further, the well-being of our society, to consider the child care profession.

It is a heavy burden. The work can be difficult. Children will challenge you as an individual. The responsibility of your profession can be weighing. However, the outcome can be rewarding beyond words. Nothing is greater than to see the effects of your work grow and prosper in a young person.

There is one other very important thing about working with children. In addition to playing an "essential" role in society, it can also be a great deal of fun!

Rod Hofstedt
Executive Director
Adults & Childrens Alliance

INTRODUCTION

THIS IS AN exciting time to be entering child care. When this book was first printed in 1987, changes were happening and the field of child care was growing. Today the field continues to change, grow, and develop. The Internet has helped take communication to powerful new levels, giving child care professionals across the world easier access to each other and to countless resources. More than ever before, people are ready to recognize that child care and early childhood education have a very close-knit relationship. Many communities are starting to put the emphasis on early care and education. And as the demand for child care services increases with each passing year, so does the need for developing not only the whole child, but his or her family, community, and any necessary community services as well.

Child care is not a new idea. Even in the early Roman civilization, foundling homes were established to care for abandoned children. As early as 1767, a *garderie*, or day nursery, opened for children whose mothers worked in the fields. The concept of caring for children isn't new, but the definition of child care is changing. Concerns of parents and government keep changing the emphasis of what child care is, what good child care means, and how to best provide it.

A child is defined in the *American Heritage Dictionary* as a "person between birth and puberty" (under thirteen years old). The *Webster's New Collegiate Dictionary* defines care as "a person or thing that is an object of attention, anxiety, or solicitude (attentive care and protectiveness)." Therefore, child care is giving attentive care and protection to the needs of children under thirteen years of age. A child is made up of many needs—physical, intellectual, social, emotional, and spiritual. Specialization in child care comes from concentrating on one or more of these needs with a certain age group of children. Through years of growing and maturing, the field of child care has parented many offspring: babysitters, daycare providers, nursery school teachers, center aides, assistants, and other specialists such as parent educators, family life specialists, and so on. They moved into the workplace, institutions, centers, homes, hospitals, and schools. They came with varying degrees of training and emphasis in the areas of teaching, nurturing, health, and creativity. What started out as simple child caring (as if child caring was ever simple) gave birth to "offspring" who aren't always ready to admit to their common ancestry.

In researching the child care field for this book, I explained what I was doing to a director of a preschool center that had a program using parent educators. The response was, "Wait a minute, first you talk about child care and then you ask about parent educators. I'm confused, which one do you want information on?"

That type of response wasn't uncommon, but history has proven that all these areas have evolved from the same ancestry. Each has just taken on different characteristics and matured in one area of this wide and growing field. Throughout the history of the United States, different goals and emphasis were stressed within the responsibility of child care. In order to meet these goals of education, health, parental involvement, and other special needs, programs were created.

The degrees and training in early childhood programs developed as the affluent country started demanding more and more expert ability in dealing with our most valued resource—our children. In fact, the emphasis moved away from child care to child development. According to the *American Heritage Dictionary*, to develop is to "bring, grow, or evolve to a more complete, complex, or desirable state." With our growing emphasis on education, you'll hear less about child care and more about child development.

Even though roles and responsibilities vary, one common thread still follows in and out of every job title and workplace: people in the child care field enjoy being with and working with young children. Regardless of what you call it, we are still caring for the child and the field is still child care.

1

CHILD CARE OPPORTUNITIES

YOU ENJOY CHILDREN and like to work with them. Knowing this is the first step in exploring child care careers. Next look at your skills and interests. Then you can decide what kind of education and training you will need—or are able to obtain—to accomplish your goals.

According to the *Occupational Outlook Handbook 2004–2005*, child care workers held about 1.2 million jobs in 2002. Many worked part-time. About half of all child care workers are self-employed, and most of them are family child care providers.

In previous editions of this book, the child care field was divided into three general areas: day care, educational programs, and substitutional care. But due to the diminishing line between "day care" and "educational programs," this book now divides the child care field into only two general areas: supplemental care and substitutional care. All day care and educational programs are supplemental care because the children in these programs are under the care of people other than their parents or guardians for only part of the day. Substitutional care is when the child's care and education are provided by others substituting for their parents for twenty-four hours a day because of a special need. Qualifications for working in any of these positions depend upon the state requirements and the duties or responsibilities you have within these programs.

The Children's Defense Fund's 2004 publication, *The State of America's Children*, states that even though child care programs vary significantly across the nation, successful programs do share some common basic goals. Regardless of which aspect of child care interests you, the following goals should be regarded as good standards:

1. Support a nurturing, trained, and stable staff.
2. Meet basic health, nutrition, and safety needs.
3. Foster caring relationships and cultural sensitivity.
4. Promote a variety of developmentally appropriate activities.
5. Encourage family involvement.
6. Help acquire academic, personal, and social skills.

Child care providers, sometimes called day-care providers, were originally considered responsible only for the children's basic care. Preschool teachers were responsible only for the children's educational activities. The separation in these major fields continues to diminish because of the growing knowledge that anyone who spends any amount of time with children does affect their learning, and they must also care about the children's basic needs. As good child care programs look at the whole child and that child's development and interactions with family and community, the goal will have to become caring for the developing child because a child has many needs. But for now, let's look at the broad views of supplemental care and substitutional care within the child care field.

Supplemental Child Care

Within the general category of supplemental child care are the following more specific categories: family child care, group child care, child care centers, teachers in a school setting, parent educators, early childhood educational programs, and alternative teaching styles. These child care categories are defined primarily by the type of setting, teaching method, and supervisory care provided.

The 2004 American Community Survey lists the percentage of children under the age of six with all parents in the labor force at 59.5 percent. These children have to be taken care of by somebody. Supplemental care, as stated before, is when children are under the care of people other than their parents or guardians for only part of the day. Let's take a closer look at the specific categories of supplemental care.

Family Child Care

Caring for other people's children in your own home is referred to as *family child care*. Each state has its own regulations or licensing requirements. According to the National Association of Child Care Resource and Referral Agencies' (NACCRRA) online fact sheet "Child Care in America," there are currently 300,032 regulated family child care homes operating. Requirements and standards may be expected of both the caregiver and the home. Basic facts from the National Association for Family Child Care (NAFCC) note that each state may have different regulations such as:

Maximum number of children
Maximum number of children for each age group
Type of facilities required

Training is also encouraged if not required. Caring for children in family child care may be different than informal child care. The NAFCC suggests contacting the local Child Care Resource and Referral Agency or local Family Child Care Association for information about training. You can find them either by checking the yellow pages under "child care" or by contacting the United Way.

Usually a family child care provider is a person who has his or her own preschool children. But women and men with no children or grown children also enjoy this profession. The provider usually takes care of children from the neighborhood or community. If the children are babies or toddlers, duties might include feeding, diapering, holding, and providing stimulating playthings, in addition to watching and protecting the children. The activities provided and care given to these children could be similar to what the family child care provider would provide for his or her own children. Family child care hours may vary. Hours are usually longer than the typical eight-hour day and may include odd shifts to accommodate working parents with similarly odd-hour shifts.

Professional family child care providers should be aware of children's developmental stages and needs. A variety of activities can be planned to encourage development and learning. (See the sample schedule under "Group Child Care" below.) They may read to the children, take them for walks, go to parks or the library, set up crafts and cooking experiences, go on picnics, or do anything that parents may do with their own children. Books, sharing with other caregivers, and training sessions are all good ways to find new activity ideas.

Many family child care providers get the CDA (Child Development Associate) credential for family child care providers. The CDA National Credentialing Program consists of two parts: training and assessment. To receive the credential, the applicant must be at least eighteen years old and demonstrate the requisite skills and knowledge (whether through formal training or experience) to a team of child care professionals from the Council for Professional Recognition (see Chapter 3 for more information on the CDA).

Besides physically protecting the children and providing activities, the child care providers will help encourage social, intellectual, and emotional development and growth within the family setting. They will arrange for nutritious meals and snacks and a safe place for the children to play. They will also give feedback to parents on their children's accomplishments and activities. Parents like to know if their children napped, how they are eating, and how they interact with other children, and about any new activity or skill that they learned.

Family child care is different from babysitting because child care is considered an approved in-home business. It is governed by state and local guidelines that are set up for the protection and education of the children. All states have some type of licensing or approval of in-home child care zoning, health stipulations, or standards. As with any home business, providers need to keep track of income, expenditures, and information for taxes, and they must make available a written statement on policies. It is easier to make exceptions on certain rules than to establish new ones after you start. Decide on things such as:

- What you are going to charge
- When you expect to get paid
- The hours or the days during which you are willing to take children
- What you do on holidays
- Whether you care for sick children
- A policy on late pickup charges

- Whether you will accept cloth diapers
- Your vacation policy
- Whether you have a trial acceptance policy
- What meals you will offer
- What procedure you will follow for interviewing parents

Although family child care is not always closely regulated (in some states it is much less regulated than in others), some typical qualifications would include the adult-to-child ratios: usually one adult must be available to every five children. Some states may not regulate a home if the provider cares for fewer than five or six children. Other requirements may include that the provider pass a physical exam and that basic safety and health standards and rules (keeping poisons out of reach of children, gates on the stairways, and so forth) and basic cleanliness standards for the home are observed.

Although there are people who are not licensed or approved yet give good care to children, caring for children in your home without some type of license or approval may violate the law. Contact your state licensing agency, listed in Appendix of this book, to find out what regulations and guidelines affect you.

Group Child Care

Caring for more than five children in the home might put you under group family child care regulations. Usually more rules and regulations affect the group provider than the family provider. Not all states allow group child care. Group providers may be licensed to care for more children, but they might have to hire an assistant or a helper. The adult-child ratio may vary with the ages of the children—the younger the children, the smaller the adult-child ratio.

The ratios usually are common sense. If a child is older, he or she can eat, interact, play, go to the bathroom, and do other activities with more independence. A baby or toddler is more dependent on and needs more attention and time from an adult.

Usually a group child care has more organized schedules and planned activities. Preschoolers, ages two and a half to five, are usually the best age for group activities. They enjoy organized activities and like some structure. Setting up planned (but of course somewhat flexible) schedules benefits the provider by supplying some organization. It also gives the children something structured to look forward to. Knowing what to expect in their daily routine decreases anxiety and increases a sense of belonging in children, making the transition between home and child care easier. A simple schedule may be something like this:

6:30–7:30 A.M.—children arrive, play quietly, or watch
    children's TV
7:30–8:00—breakfast
8:00–8:30—free play (variety of toys set out by provider)
8:30–9:30—arts and crafts (may include finger painting,
    playdough, coloring, and so forth)
9:30–9:45—juice break
9:45–10:45—outdoor play or large muscle play
10:45–11:30—choice of children's TV show or free play
11:30–noon—lunch
noon–12:30 P.M.—story time
12:30–2:30—naps or quiet time activities (puzzles, blocks,
    coloring, or reading)
2:30–3:00—snacks
3:00–5:00—outdoor play or free activities
    (creative/imaginative play)

If a provider is alone, a schedule has to allow time for him or her to greet the children when they come, prepare meals, set up activities, clean up after meals, make notes for parents, greet parents, and help children leave for the day. Both the family child care provider and the group family child care provider are self-employed with an in-home business.

Helper

An assistant or helper in a group child care home may also have to pass a general physical exam. Most child care workers have to sign a statement that they have not been convicted of either child abuse or neglect. All states require a background check or employment history check.

Contacting family child care homes or group family child care homes might be the quickest way to find out whether there are any positions available. The local licensing agency may be able to give you a list of current licensed or approved homes. You might have to convince a provider of the advantages of having help, such as being able to care for more children, being able to keep up with house and home a bit easier, easing the pressure of the busy times, and having another adult around to share ideas, enthusiasm, and just "adult talk."

Do your homework. What are your state's regulations? Does having a helper affect the number of children? Come with ideas for the children and with enthusiasm. But most important, listen to the provider and pick up on how you might help. If you find someone interested, you will have to interview for the job just as you would for any other position. Being a helper first is also a good way to decide whether you would enjoy operating a child care business in your own home.

Nanny

Nannies are child care specialists who work in a family home caring for the children. The International Nanny Association (INA) has adopted minimum standards for nannies. A nanny must:

- Be at least eighteen years of age
- Have completed high school or the equivalent
- Be in good health
- Have proof of up-to-date immunizations
- Where required, have proof of negative TB and/or chest x-ray tests

The INA found that nannies will usually fall into one of three categories:

1. Young, single individuals with babysitting and/or child care experience who enjoy working with children. These nannies usually look at becoming nannies for just a year or two. They are usually active, energetic, and open to the idea of sharing their homes and lives with families other than their own. These nannies may be taking a break from college or suspending a long-term commitment to another career.
2. Older, more mature people who may have raised a family of their own. They are drawn to this type of in-home child care because of positive past experiences.
3. Individuals who consider themselves child care professionals and specialists. Some have college degrees in early childhood or elementary education. Others may have completed a nanny training program. These people have entered the

career of being a nanny as a chosen profession, and they plan to continue it as a lifetime endeavor rather than just a short-lived job.

All nannies are looking for a good position with a nice family. Some nannies specialize in on-call, temporary, or emergency situations because they prefer to have more freedom. Some families want to hire nannies not only to care for the children, but also to manage the household, shop, cook, and perform other duties. First consider whether you want to work full-time or part-time. Then determine if you are willing to become a live-in nanny or if you prefer living in the privacy of your own home. Sometimes light housekeeping or some minor chores may be acceptable to you, but be clear and firm about what you will and will not do. Your primary responsibility is child care, although other skills may be needed on a family-to-family basis. You may have to be able to drive, swim, cook, help with homework, care for an infant, know first aid and CPR, and work with special-needs children. Nannies usually have to work unsupervised.

Nannies generally work forty to sixty hours each week and have two days off. Part-time nannies may be paid by the hour, with rates ranging from $7 to $20. A live-in nanny just starting in the field may earn a salary from $250 to $400 weekly, while a trained nanny working full-time may earn from $350 to $1,000 per week. In addition to a salary, live-in nannies often enjoy free room and board, two weeks paid vacation each year, paid major holidays, and sometimes even health insurance and the use of a car. A nanny's employer must also pay the employer's part of Social Security tax on his or her salary, and most states require unemployment taxes. Since benefits can vary from employer to employer, it is important to look at the whole package being offered when considering a job proposal.

Some nannies also go on vacations with the families to watch over and care for the children. They are included in outings and other family activities. Sometimes the nannies have to provide activities for children without the parents. A nanny may become part of the family, more or less, depending upon the personality and expectations of the family.

Although special training is not required for becoming a nanny, the INA encourages prospective nannies to obtain the special knowledge and skills required before assuming the responsibility of caring for any child. Nanny training programs in the United States, Australia, and New Zealand range from six-week training programs to college programs offering an associate's or bachelor's degree. The INA has also established a Nanny Credential Exam, which provides interested applicants an opportunity to earn a certificate to add to their portfolios or résumés. More information on this exam, along with links to state, national, and international placement agencies and other information valuable for those in this profession, can be found on the INA's website: www.nanny.org.

You might find a position as a nanny by answering help wanted ads in the paper listing child care, housekeeping, live-in or come-in child care, parental helper, or nanny positions. There are also agencies that advertise for help in the papers and online.

Child Care Centers

While many children are cared for in homes, there is growing acceptance for out-of-home settings. As stated before, philosophies of child care and educational programs are becoming more alike or perhaps more integrated. In fact, the terms "early childhood education" and "child care" programs are starting to be replaced with the term "early care and education."[1] With more mothers in the workforce, full-day programs are needed to care for preschool children. Parents who want educational programs may also need child care for the rest of the day. Whether the setting is geared to care or education, it must give high-quality services that meet developmental, social, emotional, physical, and cognitive needs.

Child care centers are also regulated by each state. Child care grew as a social service for working or needy parents. In the beginning it was basically a custodial program in which basic child care was provided. Child care today boasts of programs that help meet the varied developmental levels and cultural backgrounds of children. Centers hire child care teachers and assistants to organize and lead activities for children.

Teachers and assistants help nurture and teach preschool children. Children in child care centers are usually younger than five years old, unless it is a school-age program. In addition to attending to the child's basic needs, these providers facilitate activities that stimulate the children's physical, emotional, intellectual, and social growth. They help children explore their interests, develop their talents and independence, build self-confidence, and learn how to interact with others.

Providers in a center may function much like a group family child care provider, but on a larger scale. They usually operate in some type of center outside the home. These may be commercial centers, community or church centers, cooperative centers, public

---

1. Kagan, Sharon Lynn. *Excellence in Early Childhood Education: Defining Characteristics and Next-Decade Strategies.* Washington, DC: U.S. Government Printing Office, 1990, p. 7.

service centers, or on-site or near-site company centers. Each is described below.

- **Commercial centers.** These are one of the largest categories of child care centers. They are private profit-making centers such as Kindercare and Children's World. The basic model for the center was developed and then franchised. The franchised centers are often built and run the same way as the basic model, are usually well equipped, and are often housed in new buildings. They offer nutritious foods and developmental or educational activities including field trips. These centers usually provide their own training for staff.
- **Community or church centers.** These centers are another large group. These are private community, charitable, church, company, or cooperative parent centers. In these centers the emphasis is on the personal attention and affection available from the caregivers rather than on the building or the programs.
- **Cooperative centers.** These are private cooperatives where parents do most of the care and maintenance. On a smaller scale, these are called play groups. Many times they are run under the guidance of a paid director and some staff. The fees to parents are usually lower, as parents take turns serving as assistants to the paid staff or run the programs themselves. These centers are usually used by higher-income families. Parents also have to have flexible working hours so they can contribute some of their time to the centers.
- **Public service centers.** These are government-funded programs with the widest range of services available. Often, eligibility is restricted to low-income families. Parents are involved in the policies and educational programs, which include Head Start, Early Start, and state-funded literacy programs.
- **On-site or near-site company centers.** These are probably the smallest category of the centers. Companies began to provide

child care as a fringe benefit for employees. This type of center worked out beautifully in the well-built, well-thought-out centers like the Kaiser's shipyard in Oregon during World War II. These centers had well-qualified, competitively paid staff and offered an educational, recreational, and health-care program in a cheerful, well-equipped physical setting. These types of centers are growing rapidly as more companies offer child care benefits.

Staffing

The training and qualifications required of preschool workers vary from state to state. Many states have licensing requirements that regulate caregiver training, which may range from having a high school diploma to college courses or a college degree in child development or early childhood education.

The standard that many states are now requiring is a Child Development Associate credential, which is offered by the Council for Professional Recognition. Some employers may not require a CDA credential, but they may require secondary or postsecondary courses in child development and early childhood education. Experience in a child care setting may also be required. The following is a list of requirements and alternatives that you may need to qualify for positions in a child care center:

Master Teacher (Head Teacher, Lead Teacher, Chief Caregiver, or Child Care Associate)
- Complete a postsecondary certificate in child development assistant training (CDA), plus one year as an assistant teacher, plus one year in an accredited child-development program; or
- Complete two years as an assistant teacher and ninety hours in an accredited child-development program; or

- Possess other degrees and experience, and complete child-development courses

Teacher (Assistant Teacher)
- Complete a postsecondary certificate in child development assistant training (CDA); or
- Complete six months as a child care assistant (child care aide) or student teacher, plus ninety hours in an accredited child-development training course; or
- Possess other combinations of training, experience, and courses

Child Care Assistant (Child Care Aide)
- Complete a high school child care training course; or
- Complete an orientation training course in a child care center

Using alternative qualifications is very useful for an employer of a very skilled person who lacks the necessary training. However, you shouldn't count on going this route unless it is impossible to go on for training. Check your own state regulations for preferred qualifications and alternative options. As child care is becoming more professional, education and training will probably win out over alternative qualifications.

Teachers in a School Setting

As previously discussed, the distinction between early childhood care and early childhood education programs is getting harder to define. That is because the educational programs in child care centers have had to be extended to meet the needs of children in full-time child care.

Each state sets standards and requirements for adults working with young children. Experience and training are important. For kindergarten and primary teachers, a bachelor's degree is required. Your state education department or child care licensing division can describe the qualifications necessary for specific careers.

According to the National Association for the Education of Young Children's pamphlet *Careers in Early Childhood Education*, "Early childhood educators recognize that caring for children in groups requires special expertise. They have skills in setting up a safe, healthy, and stimulating environment; emphasizing good nutrition; and providing opportunities for active play, quiet play, and rest. Early childhood teachers must also know how to increase the difficulty and challenge of an activity as children gain understanding and skills." It is also important for teachers to keep records of each child's progress and discuss the children's progress and needs with the parents.

Prekindergarten teachers, nursery school teachers, or early childhood teachers may be licensed to plan and coordinate the instructional program. They address the intellectual, emotional, social, cultural, and physical needs of children in a prekindergarten classroom. The teacher usually is required to have a B.A. or B.S. degree as well as a background in prekindergarten, early childhood, preschool, or nursery educational courses that meet individual state requirements.

Associate teachers may be licensed to teach a group of children on a daily basis. They usually are under the supervision of a licensed prekindergarten teacher in a classroom. The associate may take an active part in planning and implementing the instructional program, but he or she does not assume overall responsibility for the program. An associate may have a two-year associate of arts (A.A.) degree with courses in early childhood education. An associate may be considered an aide or a technician and serve a supportive role rather than a teaching role.

Parent Educators

Another part of working in the early childhood careers is working with parents, families, or other adults. Parent educators, parent-child educators, family-life educators, family educators, or early childhood educators may be licensed to teach children or teach adults about parent-child interaction as well as to plan and coordinate the instructional program. Their program addresses the intellectual, emotional, cultural, social, and physical needs of parents and children in a family educational program.

Parent educators may be required to have a teaching license—with specialized study in teaching young children—as well as skills in working with adults. They may help parents of children observe and learn about their child's development through phases of play, observation, and discussion groups. Many preschool programs are based on similar approaches. Each program will be uniquely different as each child, parent, and educator is different. The functions of a parent educator in preschool programs may include:

Teaching children and adults
Directing and supervising programs
Serving as a resource person
Evaluating children's progress and program goals
Establishing opportunities and procedures for research

Parent educators may work in any preschool program with any age child. In fact, the parent educator may teach other adults about child care in many different areas, such as state extension work, social work, parent education programs, high school and college teaching, psychological therapy, and child advocacy.

Early Childhood Educational Programs

In educational programs such as nursery schools, the curriculums are taught by qualified teachers and assistants. Areas of curriculum and concentration of subjects vary depending upon the school, the needs of the children, the wants of the parents, and the purpose of the particular school. Curriculum items might include:

Outdoor activities
Arts and crafts
Language arts
Field trips
Visitors
Dramatic play
Creative music
Sciences
Reading
Large muscle activities
Small muscle activities
Cooking experiences
Children's literature
Math skills

A daily schedule like the one listed earlier in this chapter might be used. This schedule may also be broken down into time frames or activity groups that are called *blocks*. A full-day program may use six blocks, while a half-day program may use three or four blocks.

Time Scheduling/Activity Blocks

8:00 A.M.—indoor free play (block 1)—self-selected activities (list of choices)

8:30—arts and crafts (block 2)—teacher-instigated activities (list types of activities)

9:45—outdoor play (block 3)—self-selected activities (list of choices)

11:30—lunch (block 4)—meal period

12:30 P.M.—nap (block 5)—nap and story time

3:00—outdoor or free activities (block 6)—self-selected activities

A teacher in an early childhood education program will be expected to provide emotional support, guidance, and caring for the child just like the caregiver does in child care. But beyond that, a teacher will have to know how to instruct, facilitate learning, and evaluate results. Examples of goals and skills that a teacher might evaluate and record are:

Character
Thinking skills
Level of language and speech
Use of large muscles
Use of small muscles
Activities preferred
Social and emotional skills
Problem solving skills
Academic skills
Special needs

The training of the teacher and the concerns of parents may help determine what programs are offered in school. The program will also depend on the purpose of the school and why it was originally set up. Following are the most common programs available today.

- **Laboratory nursery schools.** These schools are found in universities, community colleges, and junior colleges and were originally set up to focus on pre-parental education, teacher training, and research. Today some of the better nurseries are in university laboratory schools. In community colleges and junior colleges, students often receive training as aides or associates for family child care, Head Start, and other centers. Laboratory nursery schools help set standards, add to knowledge about children, and allow college students to observe, participate, and learn about teaching.

- **Temporary experimental groups.** These groups are set up to test teaching methods, curricula, and theories, which are often related to problems of the disadvantaged. All of these college labs, research, pre-parental training, and child care training labs offer child care positions.

- **Parent-cooperative nursery schools.** Like parent-cooperative child care centers, these schools are organized by parents. A qualified teacher is hired, and parents take turns assisting the teacher. With qualified teachers and involved parents, good programs can be set up at less cost using parents as aides.

- **Church-sponsored schools.** These schools also can be set up at a lower cost, and their programs include religious training. Schools are often housed in the church, and members of the congregation are accepted first, if there is a waiting list. Sometimes the church schools have their own church-sponsored colleges, and teachers might be "called" through their own network. Being of the same religion or being a member of the congregation might be a requirement for teachers and staff.

• **Hospital nursery schools.** These schools are set up to help balance the emphasis in caring for the sick child. The goal is to help both nurses and doctors to understand the child as a whole person—that is, to understand a child's behavior as well as his or her physical needs.

• **Therapeutic nursery schools.** These programs include handicapped children—if the handicap isn't too severe—with non-handicapped students. It is found that the experience is good for all the children. Some of the special-needs programs are set up to give therapy to seriously disturbed children. In this therapeutic type of nursery school, specially trained teachers work with psychiatrists or psychologists.

• **Private nursery schools.** These schools may have a philosophy that differs at least in part with traditional nursery schools. They may, for example, stress one aspect of teaching, such as music or art, or an alternative teaching style, such as the Montessori Method or the Reggio Emilia Approach. Not all states have adequate standards on private schools. But like any other schools, good schools depend on good teachers and on adequate materials and facilities.

Alternative Teaching Styles: Montessori Method and Reggio Emilia Approach

In any child care home or center, a teaching method will likely be adopted to help the children learn and grow. You may want to consider one of the following alternative teaching styles as you look further into the child care field.

Montessori Method

Montessori schools offer a well-known alternative method of teaching. This program is based on careful, systematic observation of children, their needs, and their interests at each level of development. It stresses inner discipline, independent work, and the child's function as a member of society.

The teacher (or *director* or *directress* as they are called in the Montessori approach) has three main roles. One is to carefully observe the needs and interests of the child. A second is to prepare a beautiful, orderly, and stimulating environment that touches all aspects of life. The third is to match each child with appropriate activities or work. Observation is the key responsibility of the adult in the classroom.

Based on observation of needs and interests, the teacher seeks ways to help the child advance in the direction he or she wants to go. The teacher will help broaden the child's choices in areas such as the following:

- **Practical life activities.** Sewing, washing and drying dishes, or preparing food
- **Sensorial exercises.** Distinguishing shapes, sizes, textures, colors, temperatures, and sounds to develop senses
- **Musical activities.** Playing bells, singing, doing rhythm exercises
- **Mathematics.** Learning through use of concrete materials rather than abstractions
- **Art and craft activities.** Developing an awareness of color, form, texture, design, and the joy of creating
- **Science.** Caring for plants and animals and exploring gravity, flotation, magnetism, weather

- **Group activities.** Having been arranged by the teachers or by the children themselves
- **Language development.** Making sandpaper letters or enriching vocabulary using phonetic method

Reggio Emilia Approach

The Reggio Emilia Approach is yet another alternative teaching method that is becoming well known in the child care field. This approach to preschool education was first started by the schools of the city of Reggio Emilia in Italy after World War II. According to the Cyert Center for Early Education at Carnegie Mellon University in Pittsburgh, Pennsylvania, this Italian approach is primarily based on the teacher's role, types of projects, and the materials used.

The teacher's role is to learn alongside the children, provoking ideas and guiding them toward further exploration. Organization of the classroom and materials should be aesthetically pleasant, creating an environment ideal for learning. It is important for the teacher to observe and document the children's progress. This role as guide and researcher is essential. The teacher must also foster connections between home, school, and the community. Teachers using the Reggio Emilia Approach work with parents and other teachers to form a collective group of educators.

Projects are in-depth and long-term, which is thought to promote lifelong learning. The direction of the projects is guided by the team of educators. Each project should be concrete and long enough to develop over time. Project ideas often stem from children's interests. The ideas can be provoked by teachers and introduced through a variety of materials. The teachers also have a responsibility to help the children connect one idea to another and to the physical world.

The materials used in the Reggio Emilia projects should be aesthetically pleasing to the children. The materials should have variation in color, texture, and pattern. The materials should be inviting to touch and admire, inspiring further learning. The children in these child care programs are encouraged to explore first and discover for themselves. In fact, the environment around the children is thought of as the third teacher. Work tables and play areas are well thought out and often remodeled to fit specific projects. The look and feel of the classroom is given great emphasis. The children are actively encouraged to express their understanding of ideas through drawing, music, writing, sculpture, and other symbolic languages. For more information on the schools of Reggio Emilia, visit http://zerosei.comune.re.it.

Substitutional Child Care

As stated before, substitutional child care is nonparental care of a child for twenty-four hours a day because of a special need. This may be due to abuse or neglect, where children are removed from their homes for a period of time; hospitalization as a result of injury or illness; or some mental deficiency or emotional problem.

Foster Care

Foster care is a home where dependent, abused, or neglected children are placed. Foster care may be in the form of a licensed institution specifically set up for child care or a normal family approved or licensed for child care. Foster care takes over normal care of the child. It is like day care, but for twenty-four hours a day, be it for a short or long period of time. Foster parents or caregivers work closely with other service agencies such as the county social services.

Residential Treatment

Residential care provides treatment for the emotionally disturbed or mentally deficient. This care may be a state or private hospital that has a care unit for children, or it may be a group home that is licensed to care for groups of children with emotional or mental handicaps. Private homes or foster-care homes may also be used to care for such children.

Other residential care facilities may be found in schools for the deaf, for the blind, and for other physically handicapped children. Some of these may be schools where the child comes for educational training; others provide twenty-four-hour care because parents may live too far away for the child to commute.

Residential caregivers may have job categories similar to those of staff members at child care centers. There also may be other teachers and professional people involved, depending on the facility. Training or experience might reflect the type of care they are giving. One caregiver may be in an entry-level position similar to that of an aide in a child care center. Another caregiver will have more experience and training, like an associate. Yet a third caregiver will have the most experience and training. Duties would vary depending on the treatment or specialty of the center. Various professionals, such as medical workers, social workers, therapists, and so on, might also be available to address specific needs.

Hospital Child Care

Child care is also found in hospital settings for the care of sick children. Hospitals and medical experiences can be emotionally upsetting to both children and their families, and recognition of the long-lasting effects of such trauma and anxiety led to the development of the child-life specialist. Hospitals may refer to these personnel as *activity therapists*, *play therapists*, or *therapeutic recreation specialists*, but *child-life specialist* is the most widely recognized title for such health-care professionals.

According to the Child Life Council, "a child-life specialist is an individual who works in a health care setting, focusing on the emotional and developmental needs of children and families. Using play and other forms of communication, this professional member of the health care team seeks to reduce the stress associated with health care experiences and enables children and families to cope in a positive manner."

A child-life specialist establishes a relationship with the children through play, activities, and communication. The specialist selects play materials and equipment appropriate to the patient's age, health, and development. Activities are provided that encourage exploration, self-expression, and learning. These activities may help a child learn more about her or his illness or just provide a healthy distraction. Activities may be offered in groups, to individuals, at bedside, or wherever the child may be.

In addition to direct involvement with the child, specialists may help provide a positive, familiar, and secure atmosphere. They may pay a preadmission visit to the child and his or her family. They may be involved in choosing the colors of the room, furniture, toys, or music. The specialists do whatever they can to promote a comfortable and pleasant environment for the child.

These specialists work with the families to:

- Provide information, assurance, and support from admission to discharge
- Help the parents understand more about their child's illness
- Answer questions about the child's health and care

The child-life specialist has a bachelor's or master's degree with supervised experience in the health-care setting. Not all child-life specialists are graduates of universities with specialized child-life studies. Individuals with training in education, child development, psychology, and similar fields may enter the profession based on previous work experience and relevant training. However, those seeking child-life jobs should have experience working with hospitalized children. The experience is usually preferred in a supervised internship.

Specialists, regardless of their education or experience, must have the ability to assess the psychosocial needs of children and families. They must also be able to provide a therapeutic relationship and activities to meet individual needs. Child-life certification is available through the Child Life Council's Child-Life Certifying Commission.

The child-life assistant works under the direct supervision of the child-life specialist. An assistant usually holds a two-year college degree in a related field and has personal qualifications similar to the specialist. A year of teaching experience with children (infant through school age) in a group setting is preferred.

The child-life administrator will have a master's degree. Besides having a background similar to that of a specialist, the administrator will be competent in managing the programs, supervising the child-life staff, organizing resources, budgeting, maintaining interdepartmental communications, and keeping abreast of related programs in the health-care setting.

2

HISTORICAL DEVELOPMENT OF CHILD CARE

To UNDERSTAND THE scope of child care, you have to first understand the role that war, government policies, and federal funds have played in developing and increasing child care standards. Unfortunately, as our standards for child care rise and expectations increase, so do costs of facilities, materials, training, and quality staff. But even though people want and expect the best, few are willing or able to pay the price.

Early Problems and Solutions

Since the early 1800s when desperate immigrant women found it necessary to work to survive in the United States, Day Nursery and Infant Schools helped with the care of the children. By 1854 the first child care center was established in the United States in New York City at the Nursery and Child's Hospital. Mothers who were returning to work after being hospitalized were able to leave their children in the care of nurses.

Wartime contributed to changes and growth in child care centers and nurseries. In fact, the first permanent day nursery was established in 1863 because of the need for women to manufacture soldiers' clothing and clean hospitals during the Civil War. In 1898 the National Federation of Day Nurseries was founded. By 1900, 175 centers were organized in cities throughout the United States. Basic care was the intent of the child care centers or nurseries.

Major changes in child care started in the 1920s. Emphasis started to shift from protective care to concern for education and quality care. Caseworkers, teachers, health workers, and other professionals combined their efforts to provide better care for children. But even with the backing of these professionals, attempts to improve the quality of child care failed.

In a study by the Philadelphia Association of Day Nurseries in early 1927, it was found that care in nurseries was not adequately meeting the needs of the parents. The major complaints were inflexible hours, quarantine problems, and the exclusion of children suffering from minor illnesses.[1]

In response to the needs of parents, family child care was introduced in Philadelphia in late 1927. Many of the complaints listed about the inflexibility of care in centers were eliminated by putting children into private homes. In family care the hours and the type of care were extremely flexible. But adding an alternative type of care didn't do away with either care centers or their problems. Regardless of complaints, nurseries expanded slowly until 1931, when about eight hundred nurseries had been established.

1. *Mothers for a Day: The Care of Children in Families Other than Their Own.* Washington, DC: U.S. Government Printing Office, 1946, p. 3.

Depression Brings Federal Funding

The Great Depression in the 1930s at first had a negative effect on child care centers and nurseries. With the increased unemployment, many mothers were forced back into their homes. With fewer mothers working, the need for child care decreased. With limited enrollment and decreased funds, many centers were forced to close. By 1934 there were only 650 centers in operation.

Until the Depression era, no federal monies were used to fund child care programs. But child care got a major boost on October 23, 1933. The Federal Emergency Relief Administration (FERA) authorized funds to provide wages for unemployed teachers, nurses, nutritionists, and other workers who had been forced onto relief assistance. Many child care centers were created to employ these workers.

By January 1934 thirty states had organized emergency nurseries. In 1937 the Work Projects Administration (WPA) program, which was in charge of setting up the centers, found it had forty thousand children in attendance in the centers in a one-month study.

These centers provided a healthy environment for children from low-income families. In fact, only low-income children were eligible to enroll. The WPA nurseries gave these children "daily health inspection, necessary medical services, well-balanced meals, play, and rest in an environment conducive to normal development."[2]

Between 1933 and 1940 the government spent more than $3 million on child care for three hundred thousand children. About three-fourths of these nurseries were housed in public school buildings. People began thinking that child care for children under five years of age should and could be done through the public school

---

2. *Final Report on the WPA*. Washington, DC: Works Progress Administration, 1944, p. 62.

systems. Even the administration of FERA suggested that nursery schools become a permanent part of public schools.[3]

It was in the 1930s that the philosophy of child care centers and nursery schools grew together. The goals for quality child care provided for educational experiences. Guidance for services in health and social services in both schools and centers helped unify child care programs.[4]

World War II and More Federal Funding

The second phase of child care development and government spending came with the United States' involvement in World War II. As men went off to war, women again were needed in the labor force. More than three million married women entered the labor force between 1940 and 1944. Many of these women had preschoolers at home. Lacking adequate child care services, increased juvenile delinquency in communities and high absenteeism at work sites surfaced as problems.

The necessity of mothers to be working outside the home demanded that arrangements be made for the care of the young children. In response, the National Conference on Day Care Children of Working Mothers met in July 1941. From that meeting concerns were discussed and child care committees were set up in many states.

It took a year—until July 1942—before funds were allocated to the U.S. Office of Education and Children's Bureau for child care.

3. Breitbart, Vicki. *The Day Care Book: The Why, What, and How of Community Day Care.* New York: Alfred A. Knopf, 1974, p. 27.

4. Baker, Katherine Read. *The Nursery School: Human Relationships and Learning,* sixth ed. Philadelphia: W. B. Saunders Company, 1976, p. 32.

They designated $400,000 for child care centers and educational programs for children of working mothers in war-related industries. Grants were made available for states to establish extended school services and for welfare agencies to set up child care centers as well as other services for children of working mothers.[5]

Another $6 million were allocated in July 1942 to WPA for the purpose of reorganizing its nursery school program to meet the child care needs of employed mothers. WPA was abolished by presidential order in 1942, but the project was then funded by federal monies through the Lanham Act.[6] Congress had passed a Community Facilities Bill (known as the Lanham Act), which provided $150 million for facilities (including child care centers) that were needed in the recently expanded war-industry areas.

In less than a year, by June 1943, thirty-nine states had fully operating extended school services. In July 1945 the services peaked with 1.6 million children enrolled in nursery schools and child care centers receiving federal funds.[7] Many centers were built and staffed by professionals and volunteers who considered long hours their contribution to the war efforts.

Industry's Hand at Child Care

The public programs were supplemented by large industrial firms that were manufacturing war equipment. Some industries provided child care for their employees. Child care needs that were met were immediate and essential, including food, rest, and shelter. Although

5. Kadushin, Alfred. *Child Welfare Services*. New York: Macmillan Company, 1967, p. 304.

6. Ibid.

7. Breitbart, p. 27.

some centers were well equipped, others often offered minimal pay, lack of materials and furniture, and a low-skilled staff. Conditions were less than ideal, but it was wartime, and mothers at least knew that their children were safe.

During this time, child care workers were concerned only with basic care. They were too busy to be concerned about emotional needs or self-fulfillment. The day was filled by making sure that the children were fed and rested, checked for diseases, and appropriately clothed.[8]

Some of the better centers were run by the Kaiser shipyards, which were located in Oregon. James L. Hymes Jr., who was the director of the Child Service Department of the Kaiser Company, believed that the answer to industrial child care had to include the following:[9]

- Industries that need women to work in their plants must help with the care of their children.
- Centers should be located near or on the way to where the parents work.
- The child care facilities must be pleasant.
- Specialists should be hired, and they should be allowed to run the program.
- A framework should be set up so the needs of the community are met; skills should be used so the needs of the children are adequately met.

---

8. Braun, Samuel J., and Esther P. Edwards. *History and Theory of Early Childhood Education.* Worthington, Ohio: Charles A. Jones Publishing Company, 1972, p. 169.

9. Ibid.

Federal Funding Spreads Benefits of Centers

The federally funded programs reached a peak in July 1944 with the enrollment of 129,357 children in 3,102 centers. Except for New Mexico, every state had requested and received federal funds under the Lanham Act to operate and maintain child care programs. Fifty-two million dollars in federal funds were spent. Despite the lack of physical accommodations and the shortage of adequately trained personnel, between 550,000 and 600,000 children received care under this act.[10]

The federal funding made child care resources available to many communities that couldn't otherwise have supported centers on their own. The knowledge about child care centers and their advantages became widespread. The Children's Bureau urged local communities to establish planning committees to help ensure that these centers would continue to grow.

War Ends: Funds Withdrawn

Mothers who used the centers had organized and planned for long-term programs, but the war came to an end and so did the federal funds. With the shortage of jobs, mothers again returned to their homes. Adding the reduced numbers of working mothers to the already present shortage of trained personnel and high costs of operations, centers started closing.

On September 1, 1945, with the end of the war, industrial centers such as the Kaiser Child Service Centers shut down as quickly

10. Employed Mothers and Child Care. Washington, DC: U.S. Department of Labor, 1953, pp. 9, 19.

as they had opened. The Lanham Act was terminated and federal funds were removed. Child care centers all around the country closed. Only California managed to maintain its public centers on a large-scale basis without federal funding.

Effects of Wartime Changes on Child Care

The Woman's Bureau evaluated some of the benefits of the wartime child care experience. The agencies and general public had become more aware of the problems of the working mothers and the communities' responsibilities in helping them. Employers also agreed that the public centers helped reduce absenteeism and turnover in the plants. However, probably the most lasting effect was brought about by the cooperation of the education and welfare agencies. They were able to better understand each other's policies and goals. Also, it created greater public understanding of these agencies' standards.[11]

Since World War II there has been a slowly growing but constant concern about child care for working mothers. The Korean conflict temporarily accelerated the desire to do something about child care services. But the conflict wasn't long enough to make an impact on the growing needs in child care.

It is said that in crisis, change is most easily made. But unlike the time of a national crisis like World War II, guidelines for child care couldn't be set without national approval. High costs, higher consumer expectations of standards, long hours, and staff expectations now became serious obstacles. Conditions acceptable in wartime were no longer going to be tolerated.

---

11. Ibid., p. 20.

Child Welfare Adopts Child Care Concerns

Between 1950 and 1960 the affluent American people began asking for a policy statement concerning the role of children and family. They believed that environment may directly affect a child's intelligence. But a lack of any policy toward the issues of child care and child welfare caused concern.

In 1960 the National Conference for Day Care for Children was jointly sponsored by the Children's Bureau (U.S. Department of Health, Education, and Welfare) and the Women's Bureau (U.S. Department of Labor). The conference endorsed child care as an important part of child-welfare services in every community. The newly formed National Committee for the Day Care of Children set goals to do the following:[12]

Evaluate the need for service

Stimulate exchange of information, ideas, and experiences

Promote standards for good child care

Federal Funds for Approved Facilities

Federal funds again were earmarked for child care through a 1962 Public Welfare Amendment. This time it stipulated that it would only support those facilities that were licensed or approved by state agencies. States would also have to provide matching funds. To qualify for federal aid for child care, the states had to include the following in their child care service plans:[13]

---

12. Kadushin, p. 306.

13. "Day Care in 1963," Newsletter of National Committee for the Day Care of Children, Inc. 3 (January 1963).

- Cooperative arrangements with health and educational agencies for children receiving child care services
- Safeguards to ensure provision of child care only when it is in the best interest of the child and mother and only when need for care exists
- Payment of fees by clients who are financially able to pay all or part of the costs of care
- Priority given to members of low-income groups as well as to those geographical areas that have the greatest need for more child care

Head Start

Federal funds were strained with the onset of the costly Vietnam War, and spending priorities had to be made. So the 1960s and 1970s brought a tentative commitment by the federal government to offer early childhood education to poverty-level families.

The 1964 War on Poverty program was based on the theory that education was the solution to poverty. Before this, it was thought that changing the environment would eliminate poverty. The Community Action Program (CAP) was set up as one part of the War on Poverty policy. It was to aid communities in planning and administering their own assistance programs for the poor. Head Start emerged from this program.

Until the Head Start era, the type of preschool program available was too often determined by economic class. The disadvantaged children were housed in programs that were based primarily on custodial care. Nursery programs for the middle-class children were designed to guide them through stages of social and emotional maturation. Only the upper-class children had programs to stimulate intellectual growth.

The Head Start programs began in 1965 in response to the government's commitment to offer early childhood education to families who were living at the poverty level. The intent was to involve the parents rather than create an educational program. Program leaders believed that it was important to the success of these programs to start where the child was, with support for the parents' beliefs and concerns. In addition, supportive services were offered as needed.

The Head Start Difference

Head Start differed from the simple definition of a nursery school, whose chief purpose was to provide educational services to preschool children. It also offered more than the care and protection that child care provided. Head Start became a forerunner of a special type of child care educational program that added the emphasis of parental support and involvement. Three phrases that set this program off from the others were community control, compensatory education, and parental enrichment.[14]

As the federal funds gradually diminished in the 1970s, the support from the community (by providing services or use of community buildings) made the difference in many programs either becoming successful or closing their doors. Many parents, professionals, and volunteers became involved with the programs.

The purpose of Head Start was to give preschoolers the experiences they need in preparation for school. It was designed to help children who had limited firsthand experiences in play activities, who had limited exposure to books, or who lacked competence in using the English language.

---

14. Braun, pp. 176–77.

This program plan included checking for and correcting physical defects in hearing, vision, and other physical conditions. It would help a child feel confident and gain self-respect. It would also help the child acquire social skills and a good background for concept development and reading readiness. In the home-based program, the teacher visits the home and instructs the parents in ways to guide and stimulate cognitive growth—the process of acquiring knowledge. The program grew to include mentally handicapped children.

Innovative Programs

In the 1960s, math and science programs were extended down into kindergarten classes. Many children who had a difficult time learning the basic skills of reading couldn't cope with the new abstractions. Realizing this was a growing problem, the developmental and educational psychologists turned their interests and research to cognition and learning in the early years. The federal government, concerned and influenced by this process, began supporting innovative programs for young children.

In 1969 the Office of Child Development was added to the Department of Health, Education, and Welfare. The purpose was to take a comprehensive approach to the development of young children and to combine programs that dealt with the physical, social, and intellectual aspects of child care.[15]

As the child care programs expanded in the late 1960s, the concept of the Child Development Associate (CDA) grew. During the 1960s mothers again returned to work. This time the women's lib-

---

15. Baker, p. 35.

eration movement demanded that women should have the freedom to pursue careers. This meant that quality child care was needed for all children. Head Start programs for the economically disadvantaged preschoolers grew, but licensed child care centers also spread rapidly.

The late 1960s was a period in which research indicated the importance of good early child care for later development. But as child care numbers increased, no guidelines were established for quality in child care. Parents and professionals alike began calling for higher standards in child care programs.

In 1970 the Administration for Children, Youth, and Families (ACYF) of the Department of Health, Education, and Welfare committed itself to the quality of child care by focusing on the competence of the child care staff. This ACYF task force set national goals to:[16]

- Identify basic skills needed by staff to provide competent care
- Provide training for caregivers in these competency areas
- Evaluate the work of caregivers on a national standard and recognize them with a national award or "credential"—the CDA

In 1972 several early childhood education and child development associations established a nonprofit consortium. They developed and carried out a system of evaluating and credentialing child care workers. The Child Development Associate would be awarded

---

16. "Family Day Care Providers: Child Development Associate Assessment Systems and Competency Standards." Washington, DC: CDA National Credentialing Program, 1985, p. 53.

based on the goals set by the ACYF task force. In 1973 the Head Start supplementary training was converted to a CDA orientation, with colleges and universities participating across the country.

CDA assessments were made available to child care workers serving three- to five-year-olds in center-based programs. Between 1983 and 1985 the assessments were expanded to include caregivers, in-home visitors, and family child care providers, as well as center caregivers working with infants, toddlers, and handicapped children. Field testing was set up and was successful.

The National Association for the Education of Young Children (NAEYC) entered into a forty-two-month agreement with the Administration for Children, Youth, and Families (ACYF). They assumed management of the CDA program. The NAEYC set up a separate nonprofit corporation called The Council for Early Childhood Professional Recognition. This administering council took effect September 1, 1985.

Today the field-based CDA training is conducted by child care programs, Head Start centers, independent consultants, and more than three hundred colleges and universities. Candidates who are applying for assessments must have at least three educational experiences in some type of early childhood education or child development courses. An applicant must choose one CDA assessment in a center-based setting: preschool (ages three to five years) or infant/toddler (up to three years old). Family child care providers and home visitors are assessed on their work with families and children in their care.

It was discovered that the most significant gains were made in federally funded child care programs when all the goals were clearly understood. The leadership in these programs should be drawn from people trained in early childhood education, and an adequate supply of resources must be available. It was also noted that the experiences offered to children should be appropriate to their developmental levels.

Head Start was given credit for widening the acceptance of group experiences of children under six years of age. It helped to improve the understanding of what good education for young children really is and underscored the need for change in the primary school programs. Also recognized was the need for adequately trained teachers or caregivers in all programs.

States Given Block Grants

In the early 1980s the Department of Health and Human Services proposed child care regulations that would deal with many standards in child care centers. Ratios of staff and children, training qualifications for caregivers, nutritional guidelines, health care, parent involvement, and the size of a group were all to be regulated.

Before this came into effect, the Social Service Block Grant Act was enacted. This act amended federal requirements dealing with Title XX–funded child care centers. In effect, if states or local governments had standards already in operation, they would be "grandfathered in" over the federal guidelines. It was thought that state and local guidelines would be set lower than were the federal guidelines.

In a study done on guidelines, many written standards were indeed set lower or were nonexistent. But most states were actually in compliance with federal guidelines or even surpassed them in practice. But with more federal cutbacks, states feared that they wouldn't be able to maintain standards even if they existed. Under the Block Grant, states gained major responsibilities for setting and enforcing standards of health, safety, and the developmental needs of children in child care.

Similarly, in the Education Consolidation and Improvement Act of 1981, Chapter 2, the U.S. Department of Education's involvement with early childhood education was consolidated into the program of block grants to each state and its local educational agencies. Thus the states and local educational agencies have the discretion and flexibility to initiate and support services for early childhood education. Federal control and guidance were given to the states.

The Handicapped Act

The Handicapped Act Amendments (Public Law 99-457) Part H—Handicapped Infant and Toddler was enacted in October 1986. By September 1989 all fifty states were involved in the Part H program. Part H targets children from birth to age two who would have substantial developmental delays if intervention services were not provided. It was to assist each state to develop a statewide, comprehensive, coordinated, multidisciplinary interagency system to provide early intervention services for handicapped infants and toddlers and their families.

Smart Start

The Community Collaborative for Early Childhood Development Act of 1989 provided funding to upgrade, expand, and create high-quality early childhood development programs for children.[17] These

---

17. United States Congress. *Smart Start: The Community Collaborative for Early Childhood Development Act of 1989*. Washington, DC: U.S. Government Printing Office, 1989.

funds were focused on the children the year before they entered kindergarten, usually at four years of age.

Smart Start stated that children who participate in such programs realize long-lasting effects in that they are:

- Less likely to need remedial education
- More likely to graduate from high school and to obtain jobs or go on to higher education
- Less likely to be dependent on welfare, and
- Less likely to be involved in a teenage pregnancy or criminal activity

The economic benefits were seven dollars saved for every dollar spent. The purpose of the bill was to increase the availability of high-quality, full-day, full-year, developmentally comprehensive and appropriate early childhood programs. Also, it was to promote coordination of resources for and among agencies and organizations that provide early childhood development services.

Smart Start was to be available to existing programs such as Head Start and school-based programs. Also, it was to be available for programs where any of the important characteristics were missing. Smart Start identified the following as important characteristics of a good early childhood development program:

Low child-adult ratio (10:1)
Small group size (maximum 20)
Developmentally appropriate curriculum
Parental involvement
Parent education
Social, health, and nutritional services
Trained staff

The 1990 Child Care Bill

In 1990 the U.S. Congress passed a comprehensive child care legislation. Through the Child Care and Development Block Grant and amendments to Title IV-A of the Social Security Act (At-Risk Child Care), child care funds were available. These funds were to help families with child care costs and help states improve quality and numbers of child care services. Congress also reauthorized Head Start to expand its early childhood development program to serve all eligible children by 1994.

Seventy-five percent of these funds ($1.5 billion in grants for direct services to poor families through Title IV-A of the Social Security Act and $2.5 billion in child care and development grants mostly for the working poor) were intended to help families pay for child care. The remaining 25 percent of the block grant was reserved for quality improvements, early childhood education, and school-age child care programs. It had other features:

- It required states to designate a lead agency to direct child care programs.
- It required states to set health and safety child care standards.
- It allowed eligible families to choose any licensed provider such as Head Start, churches, schools, or family child care.

Starting in fiscal year 1992, $50 million annually was to be authorized to help states improve licensing and registration requirements and to monitor and enforce licensing requirements for programs servicing children. Half of this amount was to be used for training. Before being able to use these monies, each state would have to do the following:

- Form a broad-based advisory group
- Select an appropriate lead agency to locate and coordinate as many different programs as possible
- Monitor compliance to supplement, not supplant, other funds
- Promote common policies and practices in all programs
- apply basic protection to all children in licensed or regulated care
- Create a statewide resource and referral agency that services all families
- Use funds to help families pay for child care
- Establish sliding fee scales that are fair and realistic

The Beginning of a New Perspective

The changes and attitudes toward child care and education started to take form at the president's September 1989 education summit. Emphasized were:[18]

Setting national goals
Making a commitment to early intervention
Linking societal and educational concerns

A fourth "r" was added to the reading, 'riting, and 'rithmetic drill: "Readying children to function optimally in an increasingly stressful and technologically sophisticated society."

---

18. Kagan, Sharon L. *Excellence in Early Childhood Education: Defining Characteristics and Next-Decade Strategies.* Washington, DC: U.S. Government Printing Office, 1990, pp. 1–3.

Social, emotional, and functional goals were added to the traditionally cognitive competence in education. Furthermore, educational goals included, as appropriate, involvement in:

Preventing problems before they began
Working with young children
Supporting families in their complex roles
Collaborating with other community institutions

These goals not only reflected a major change in the educational system, but they also highlighted changing attitudes toward the care and education of young people in our country.

No Child Left Behind Act

In 2001 the No Child Left Behind Act (NCLB) was established, bringing quality education to the forefront of America's minds. President Bush expressed deep concern that too many of the neediest children were being "left behind." According to the executive summary, archived on www.ed.gov, this act includes a "framework on how to improve the performance of America's elementary and secondary schools while at the same time ensuring that no child is trapped in a failing school." The four pillars of NCLB are:[19]

1. **Stronger accountability for results.** This requires schools to take corrective actions to improve their students' ability to achieve academic proficiency.

---

19. U.S. Department of Education. "Four Pillars of NCLB" and "Executive Summary." *Introduction: No Child Left Behind.* Washington, DC, on the Internet at www.ed.gov/print/nclb/overview/intro.

2. **More freedom for states and communities.** This allows individual states and communities to determine how to best use federal education funds.
3. **Proven education methods.** This allocates federal funding for scientifically based programs and teaching methods that work to improve student learning and achievement.
4. **More choices for parents.** This gives parents of children in low-performing schools more options, such as having their children transferred to a better performing school or to receive supplemental educational services (tutoring, after-school services, and summer school).

Good Start, Grow Smart Early Childhood Initiative

With the No Child Left Behind Act paving the way, the government's focus on early education became a natural progression. In 2002 President Bush announced "Good Start, Grow Smart: The Bush Administration's Early Childhood Initiative." The initiative was launched to help states and local communities strengthen early learning programs for young children. It was clear that young children needed to be better equipped with the skills they needed to start school ready to learn. This initiative addresses three main areas:[20]

---

20. The White House. Executive Summary: "Good Start, Grow Smart: The Bush Administration's Early Childhood Initiative." Washington, DC, on the Internet at www.white house.gov/infocus/earlychildhood/sect1.html.

1. **Strengthening Head Start.** This ensures quality education is being provided in these government-sponsored child care programs.
2. **Partnering with states to improve early childhood education.** This allows more flexibility with federal child-care funds and provides caregivers with education guidelines that align with state K–12 standards.
3. **Providing information to teachers, caregivers, and parents.** This closes any gap between the best research and current practices in early childhood education.

Conclusion

With continual government backing and financial support, opportunities should be plentiful in the continuously growing field of child care and education. This is an exciting time to be entering the child care field. Unfortunately, many of the problems faced by child care workers in the past are still facing child care workers today. But improvements have been made and continue to be made. Low self-esteem, low pay, poor working conditions, and few benefits are some of the areas being looked into and tackled by support groups, unions, and child care organizations. Improved educational standards and a general upgrading of the profession and professionals is also underway. With increasing standards for child care programs will come increasing standards for child care workers. As standards continue to rise for child care workers, more personal and professional attributes will be expected.

3

Qualifications and Training

Child care careers cover an extremely wide scope of services. Child care may include nurturing, teaching, or caring for children with special needs. It may be a business located in your own home, in a center, in a school, in a church, at a work site, in an institution, or in a hospital. You may aid a caregiver as a helper, be a caregiver, assist a teacher, be a teacher, or be a part of a health, welfare, or educational professional team. Let's take a closer look at what qualifications are needed and how to gather more information on areas that interest you.

Personal Qualifications

In child care more than in other fields, you have to really know yourself. The time to evaluate your abilities, interests, and goals should come before you commit yourself. You may get a job babysitting, but working toward a career in child care demands a much bigger commitment. Child care can be very consuming and emotionally draining. Are the rewards worth it? That all depends upon what you consider to be rewarding.

Are high pay, status, benefits, socialization, and excellent working conditions important rewards? Although great strides are being made, low pay, isolation, few benefits, and poor working conditions still confront many child care workers. Many are uniting to combat these problems. (See Chapter 6.)

Job conditions and benefits vary from work site to work site. A child-life specialist in a large hospital may expect better working conditions and benefits than a child care aide in a small neighborhood center. If these types of rewards are important to you, consider carefully the type of training you get and the work site you choose. Education, training, and location are all factors that will help determine your working conditions and benefits.

Many rewards for people in the child care field come in other ways. Rewards include the pride in seeing a child blossom, grow, and express herself or himself. Rewards are learning something about yourself, seeing what you learned in theory come alive and feeling good about a child's new discovery. Rewards are gained from your own personal growth and understanding. If these are rewards for you, then you will find child care rewarding.

Are You Interested?

After reading about child care jobs in Chapter 1, you should have some idea of what kinds of jobs are available. But how do you know if you really are suited for child care? Are you demonstrating an interest in child care by the things you like to do and by who you are? Answer the following questions to get a good idea of your aptitude for this field.

Do you love little children?
Are you mature enough to handle crises?
Do you like closeness?
Are you open to new ideas?
Are you patient?
Do you have lots of energy?
Do children like you?
Do you like babysitting and playing with children?
Do parents of the children you care for like you?
Can you relate one-to-one with children?
Do you like to learn and teach?
Do you like arts, crafts, music, and reading?
What kinds of work have you done and enjoyed?

Think about what you do in your life. What things do you enjoy doing for hobbies or for fun? What kinds of part-time, volunteer, or full-time jobs have you had? What kinds of things do you enjoy? Make a list. Does your list complement a person who works with children? Not everything will, of course, but generally do you like doing things that are similar to the duties of a child care worker?

The younger you are the fewer experiences you might have had, but if you are younger, consider these questions: Do you babysit, volunteer as a candy striper at the hospital, enjoy crafts, have patience to help others, or just enjoy spending time with younger children? What courses did you enjoy in school?

Some related or helpful experiences are babysitting, first aid courses, and crafts. Interest may be shown in volunteer experiences in child care centers, schools, institutions, hospitals, or camps. Related school subjects that you might take are child care, first aid, home economics, health, nursing care, psychology, and sociology.

Are You Capable?

Caring for children might seem like a simple job physically until you think of your job duties. Some physical limitations may be acceptable in larger centers, schools, or special situations. You may have to lift children, chairs, or tables, or you may have to move other objects. You have to bend over and crouch down while interacting with the children, whether you are teaching them skills, getting them dressed, or helping them pick up and put away toys or projects. Usually you need good movement in your arms (to hug and carry), hands (to cut and demonstrate), and fingers (to mold, color, and point). You need to be able to communicate and to demonstrate correct use of the language, to hear children's questions, and to see what they are doing and to distinguish colors and shapes for their learning. So, personal qualifications are quite inclusive.

Here are some other qualifications necessary to do this type of work:

• **Physical qualifications.** Are you physically capable of carrying; lifting; seeing; hearing; moving fingers, arms, and hands; speaking; and getting from one place to another quickly?

• **Emotional qualifications.** Are you emotionally stable enough to control your temper; to be nurturing, caring, and loving; and to be prepared to handle crises? Do you have patience and and are you committed?

• **Social qualifications.** Are you able to withstand both the closeness on the work site with children and the isolation from other adults? Do you have the interpersonal skills for communication, exchanging ideas, and getting along with others?

• **Intellectual qualifications.** Are you able to understand and follow instructions? A child care worker in any specialization should know the basic skills that the children are learning and be able to help the children learn. The worker should also be able to help develop an environment conducive to learning. Knowledge can be learned. To be a child care worker, you don't have to know everything to enter the field, but you have to be capable of and interested in learning it.

Degrees of Preparation

How much training and education do you need to get the job that you want? You might be able to get a job as an aide in a child care center right out of high school or perhaps even if you had to drop out. But being able to enter the field in this way is becoming harder and harder as more people are taking vocational technical training to learn skills to be an aide. If you were a manager for a child care center and needed to hire an aide for an entry-level position, who would you hire—a high school graduate or a child development graduate from a nine-month vocational school?

Both might be willing to work at the same wage. But the one who took the child development training program obviously was planning on a career and has an eye on the future. The high school graduate might have good references and be willing to work, but training will win out in a choice between an obviously trained and committed individual and an individual with little training. The choice will not be made because of personality but because of better qualifications.

Financial needs or other responsibilities might determine which route you take. Some routes may seem slower than you want, but there are benefits in any one you choose. The more training you have, the more qualified you are for higher paying and responsible positions. But the experience you get before you graduate will help determine which specialty you are best suited for and make you more qualified in the long run.

Setting Career Goals

What do you eventually want to be doing in the child care field? Check and see what qualifications you need to get there. Are there alternative means (experience plus educational training)? We have already explored what kinds of jobs are available, what the duties are, and where these jobs are located. Now as you are thinking about goals, let's explore some sample training courses and what knowledge you might have to learn. States differ in requirements, and even schools within states may vary in what they teach. See Chapter 9 of this book for information on community/vocational/technical schools and colleges.

When you set goals, think of the whole picture. Where are you now? Where do you want to be? Are there different ways to get there? How much time, money, and education do you want, or how much are you able to spend to get there? Do you see yourself as a child care provider—a nurturer, a role model, a developmental guider? Do you see yourself as a teacher—an instructor, a presenter of materials and ideas? Do you see yourself as an educator working with families and instructing in child development? Or perhaps you want to interact and help families and children work out problems in the role of a therapist. Do you see yourself in a health-care setting easing the trauma for children and their families over fears and concerns about their illness and treatment?

The child care field is exciting because of the variety of positions and degrees of responsibility. If you want to work with children, there is probably a position that will be right for you. As we explore the training requirements, keep in mind what you want to be doing and how you see yourself, your goals, and your personality.

On-the-Job Training

Hiring a person for on-the-job training may be a little risky. This person is probably coming in with little or no work experience. On-the-job training, however, is also a great way for people who can't otherwise get the needed training to prove themselves with supervised work experience. As with other new employees, a probationary or trial period might be in effect throughout the training period. This trial period is usually set for a definite period of time, generally from one to six months.

The training might include a period of observation, actual classroom instruction, one-to-one supervision, or just working closely with a long-time employee. If formal schooling isn't the direction for you, this is an excellent way to obtain needed training. In fact, if you don't have experience or training, stating on your application that you are willing and eager to get additional training provided by the center or institution will help express your commitment.

Child Care Providers

All states have regulations concerning family child care homes and centers. Family child care homes may be licensed, approved, certified, or registered by individual states. Individuals wanting to provide child care in their homes must meet certain safety and health standards. They might also be required to pass a physical exam. Family child care providers might have other requirements, such as child-adult ratios, hours of training, basic house cleanliness, and guidelines concerning the care and protection of children.

Since family child care and group family child care are small in-home businesses, here are some other necessary qualities:

Talent for working with children
Sense of humor
Self-starter personality
Good organizational skills
Physical stamina
Emotional stability
Consistency
Creativity
Ability to handle finances
Ability to handle a flow of customers
Mind for business
Communication skills
Good mental attitude
Good discipline

For other state requirements contact your state's licensing agency listed in the Appendix. Both the provider and the home have to meet standards. Licensing or approval may have to be reevaluated each year with a home visit by a licensing representative. A number of training hours accumulated and perhaps a review of your records also may be required.

A provider has to keep records of children in care, records for the food program if they are involved in one, and records of income and expenditures for tax purposes. (The food program is explained in more detail in Chapter 7.) A provider has to set the working hours (which will depend on needs of the parents), rates (which have to be competitive with other providers), policies, and services (which will or will not be provided).

A provider has to advertise for potential families as well as interview them, provide nutritious meals and snacks, plan activities appropriate to ages, and supervise play activities. A provider has to learn to balance the day's duties to allow time for cooking and cleanup in addition to the care and supervised play activities for a number of preschool-aged children. Organization and planning are important skills for a smoothly run program.

Community/Vocational/Technical Assistant

Nine- to twelve-month programs for a child development assistant or aide are offered at vocational schools. These programs help qualify a person for positions in the following:

Licensed or approved family child care
Foster homes
Early childhood centers
School-age care
Group homes
Developmental achievement centers
State and private hospitals
School settings (aides, school attendants)
Private homes (nannies, attendants, governesses)

To find out what type of child care development training or early childhood education is offered in your state, contact your state office of higher education (see Chapter 9) or your high school counselor.

The following is an example of a child care development program and the type of courses and requirements it may include. This information is from the Directory of Courses of Minnesota.

Areas of Knowledge

Instruction is included in areas of child growth and development, nutrition program planning and management, safety and behavior guidance, recreational and play activities, child abuse and neglect, parent-child personal relationships, learning experiences for children, interpersonal relationships, and laws, regulations, and policies relating to child care services.

Personal Qualifications

Qualifications basic to most child care positions are emotional maturity, interpersonal skills, stamina, patience, ability to work with people in stressful situations, openness to personal growth, above average reading skills, and a commitment to children.

Sample Program Description

This may include the following:

Participation with groups of young children
Child growth and development
Creative activities
Workshops
Family development and relationships
Nutrition, health, and safety of young children
Social problems
Personal and vocational preparation

Practicum

Practical field experiences might be offered in the following:

Licensed family child care
Early childhood centers
Special education
Elementary education
State hospitals
Residential centers or homes

Individuals coming out of this course might accept positions as a nanny or child care center aide or assistant, go to work as a family child care provider, or decide to work with handicapped children in schools, groups, institutions, or facilities. These child care workers will usually be working under the supervision of professional personnel. Therefore, the ability to follow instructions and to work independently as well as part of a team is important. In a child care center, this person might qualify for a position as an aide or an assistant teacher and work under the guidance of the lead teacher and director to carry out the program activities. A graduate might also be qualified for a second level residential caregiver position.

Two-Year Associate Training

A two-year community/technical college or child development training program may qualify a person for a third level of residential care or lead teacher in a child care center. The two-year associate training program should be a combination of instruction and practicum. It can lead to an Associate of Arts (A.A.) degree and can prepare an individual for the Child Development Associate (CDA) credential.

Most of these associates will work with young children in groups. The associate may oversee activities in storytelling, outdoor play, organized games, field trips, and communication skills and in creative areas such as arts and music. Some associates may work in institutions or hospitals with handicapped, sick, or injured children.

Personal Traits

Special personal qualities should include the following:

Interest in children
Ability to relate to children
Maturity
Organization
Patience
Creativity
Self-motivation
Planning

Sample Course Work

Course work for a two-year associate degree will include general education requirements along with a concentration in child development (early childhood education) training classes as well as field experience.

Fall 1st Year	*Fall 2nd Year*
Introduction to Early Childhood Education	Infants and Toddlers Music

Child Care and Guidance
Introduction to College
  Writing
Child Development I
Observation I
Early Childhood Practicum

Issues in Cultural Diversity
Outdoor Activities for Children
Guiding Behaviors
Early Childhood Practicum

Winter 1st Year
Children's Literature
Infants and Toddlers
Family, Food, and Nutrition
Health and Safety for the
  Preschool Child
Creative Activities I
Early Childhood Practicum

Winter 2nd Year
Children Under Stress
Computer Science
English
Social Science
Parent-School-Community
  Relations
Early Childhood Practicum

Spring 1st Year
Curriculum I
Math
Child Development II
Exceptional Child
Observation II
Creative Activities II
Early Childhood Practicum

Spring 2nd Year
Physical Education
Health
Infant and Toddler
  Environments
Parent Relations
Cooperative Education
Contemporary Issues in
  Child Care
Early Childhood Practicum

What makes this program inviting is that upon completion, the associate may have a two-year Associate of Arts (A.A.) degree, which can later be applied toward a bachelor's degree. It also prepares the individual with a good background and training for working with young children and provides a good educational basis with practical experiences. How many students out of college express concern that no one will hire them without experience? With the field work in many of these child care programs, the experience is there when you graduate, along with some good recommendations.

Child Development Associate

The Child Development Associate (CDA) credentialing program is a national program that provides in-service training, assessment, and credentialing experiences. It focuses on the CDA competencies. A CDA is a person who has demonstrated the ability to meet the needs of children and adults. He or she works with parents and other adults to nurture the child's physical, emotional, social, and intellectual growth within the child's own developmental stages. This credential is awarded to individuals who successfully complete the CDA assessment process. About half the states have incorporated the credentials into their child care licensing requirements.

Credentials

A CDA credential may be obtained for any one of four settings: center-based infant/toddler, center-based preschool, family child care, or home visitor settings. Individuals in any of these settings might also obtain a specialization in bilingual training for Spanish and English.

Center-Based Settings

This will be in a state-approved child development center where the caregiver can be observed as the main provider of services to a group of children. Center-based settings may include child care, nursery schools, preschools, child-development programs, and Head Start centers. The centers have the option of one of two endorsements— either the infant/toddler (birth to thirty-six months) or preschool (children three to five years old).

Family Child Care Setting

This setting will be in a state approved or licensed family child care home. The candidate must be observed as the main provider who is caring for at least two nonrelative children under the age of five.

Home Visitor Setting

In this setting the caregiver makes regular visits to family homes. The candidate must be able to be observed working with children five years old or younger. The caregiver also works to support parents in meeting the needs of their children.

CDA Competency Standards

Following are the CDA competency goals and function areas. These are similar in all settings.

Although their content differs, the CDA Competency Standards for all settings have the same structure. The Competency Standards are divided into six competency goals, which are statements of a general purpose or goal for caregiver behavior. The competency goals are common to all child care settings.

The six goals are defined in more detail in thirteen functional areas, which describe the major tasks or functions that a caregiver must complete to meet each competency goal. Each functional area is explained by a developmental context, which presents a brief overview of relevant child development principles.

Although the six competency goals are the same for all settings (center based, family child care, home visitor), the functional area definitions and sample behaviors change to define the particular skills needed for the specific child care setting and/or age grouping.

Table 3.1, which is reproduced from "CDA Competency Standards" by permission of the Council for Professional Recognition, presents the six competency goals and the functional areas within each of them for caregiver behavior in a family child care setting.

The CDA assessment is a process by which a caregiver's competence is evaluated by the CDA National Credentialing Program. The evaluation is done by a team made up of the candidate, an early childhood professional as the advisor, a member of the community, and a CDA representative. Each of these team members observes and collects information about the candidate's work as it relates to the CDA competency standards. The candidate must prepare a personal portfolio, which includes the following:

- An autobiographical statement
- A program description
- Written examples of competency in each of the thirteen functional areas

The local assessment team makes a recommendation. The recommendation and materials are sent to the CDA National Credentialing Program. The national office reviews the material and sends the decision to the candidate. If the credential is awarded, it is valid for three years and must then be renewed every five years.

The amount of time to complete this assessment may vary. The candidate must work with the advisor for at least twelve weeks. Candidates may finish in a few months or in a year or more.

Table 3.1 CDA Competency Goals and Functional Areas for Caregivers

Competency Goals	*Functional Areas*
I. To establish and maintain a safe and healthy learning environment	1. **Safe:** Candidate provides a safe environment to prevent and reduce injuries.
	2. **Healthy:** Candidate promotes good health and nutrition and provides an environment that contributes to the prevention of illness.
	3. **Learning environment:** Candidate uses space, relationships, materials, and routines as resources for constructing an interesting, secure, and enjoyable environment that encourages play, exploration, and learning.
II. To advance the physical and intellectual capabilities of the children	4. **Physical:** Candidate provides a variety of equipment, activities, as well as opportunities to promote the physical development of competence.
	5. **Cognitive:** Candidate provides activities and opportunities that encourage curiosity, exploration, and problem solving appropriate to the various developmental levels and learning styles of children.
	6. **Communication:** Candidate actively communicates with children and provides opportunities and support for children to understand, acquire, and use verbal and nonverbal means of communicating thoughts and feelings.
	7. **Creative:** Candidate provides various opportunities that stimulate children to play with sound, rhythm, language, materials, space, and ideas in individual ways and to express their creative abilities.

(continued)

Table 3.1 (continued)

Competency Goals	Functional Areas
III. To support social and emotional development and provide positive guidance	8. **Self:** Candidate provides physical and emotional security for each child and helps each child to know, accept, and take pride in himself or herself and to develop a sense of independence.
	9. **Social:** Candidate helps each child feel accepted in the group, helps children learn to communicate and get along with others, and encourages feelings of empathy and mutual respect among children and adults.
	10. **Guidance:** Candidate provides a supportive environment in which children can begin to learn and practice appropriate and acceptable behaviors as individuals and as a group.
IV. To establish positive and productive relationships with children and their families	11. **Families:** Candidate maintains an open, friendly, and cooperative relationship with each child's family, encourages their involvement in the program, and supports the child's relationship with his or her family.
V. To ensure a well-run, purposeful program	12. **Program management:** Candidate is a manager who uses all available resources to ensure an effective operation. The candidate is a competent organizer, planner, record keeper, and communicator and is a cooperative coworker.
VI. To maintain a commitment to professionalism	13. **Professionalism:** Candidate makes decisions based on knowledge of early childhood theories and practices, promotes quality in child care services, and takes advantage of opportunities to improve competence, both for personal and professional growth and for the benefit of children and families.

Contact the national office for more information about how to apply for your CDA credential:

Council for Professional Recognition
2460 Sixteenth Street NW
Washington, DC 20009-3575
www.cdacouncil.org

According to the Council of Professional Recognition's website, the cost of an assessment application packet is $15, in addition to $5 to cover shipping and handling. The fee for the assessment itself is $325.

Prekindergarten/Nursery School Teacher

Contact the state teacher certification office for specific educational requirements for early childhood teacher certifications for each individual state. (See the Appendix.) Also, high school counselors or college placement offices can give you this information.

A prekindergarten or nursery school teacher is licensed to teach a group of children on a daily basis. The teacher will plan and coordinate the instructional program to meet the intellectual, emotional, social, cultural, and physical needs of the preschool-aged child.

The prekindergarten teacher will have to meet the state's educational requirements. Usually a teacher will have to complete a baccalaureate degree (B.S. or B.A.) from an accredited college or university plus specific course work in early childhood education, which may or may not have been part of the degree.

Examples of the types of courses needed are as follows:

Theory
Child psychology
Stages of development
Teacher-child relations
Record keeping
Family as a social and cultural unit
Child development
Curriculum
Classroom management
Styles of learning
Home-school relations

National Association for the Education of Young Children Accreditation

Since there is no teaching certificate available in many states for preschool or child care practitioners, the Child Development Associate credential was developed as an alternative. There are also other accreditation programs that ensure providers and their child care programs meet the national standards of excellence in early childhood education. (See Figure 3.1.)

The National Association for the Education of Young Children (NAEYC) is currently establishing a new accreditation system that will set a standard for associate degree programs in early education. The standards were based on research in early childhood development that describes what well-prepared graduates of two-year colleges should know and be able to do.

The NAEYC has also developed an early childhood credentialing system, but instead of being for individuals or for higher education, this accreditation is for the child care program itself. The following steps are required to reach NAEYC accreditation:

Figure 3.1 Directors in Child Care Centers

Amount of Minimum Preservice Training in Early Childhood Education and
Administrative Topics

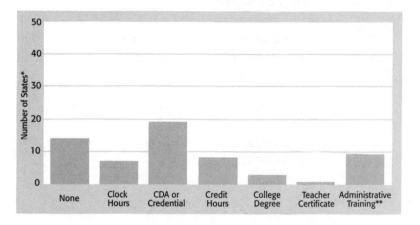

Amount of Preservice Training	Number of States*
None	14
Clock Hours	7
CDA or Credentials	19
Credit Hours	8
College Degree	3
Teacher Certificate	1
Administrative Training**	9

*States include New York City and the District of Columbia for a total of 52 entities.
**Administrative training may be in addition to early childhood education requirements.

Source: National Child Care Information Center (NCCIC). "A Snapshot in Trends in Child Care
Licensing Regulations," *Child Care Bulletin*, Issue 28, Winter 2003.
On the Internet at http://nccic.acf.hhs.gov/ccb/issue28.html#1.

1. Enroll in self study.
2. Become an applicant.
3. Become a candidate.
4. Meet the program standards.

To find out more about these steps and about the new 2006 NAEYC Early Childhood Program Standards and Accreditation Performance Criteria, contact the NAEYC:

National Association for the Education of Young Children (NAEYC)
Resources for Early Childhood Professionals
1509 Sixteenth Street NW
Washington, DC 20036
www.naeyc.org

Prekindergarten Associate

A prekindergarten associate is licensed to teach a group of children on a daily basis under the direct supervision of a licensed prekindergarten teacher in the classroom. This person would assist the teacher the way an assistant helps a lead teacher in a child care center. The difference is that here the emphasis is teaching. This associate takes an active part in planning and implementing the instructional program but does not assume overall responsibility.

The associate has to meet individual state requirements. The associate may have an Associate of Arts degree from an accredited college plus course work in the same areas that a prekindergarten teacher would have, but with fewer requirements. A lead teacher in a child care center may meet requirements of a teacher-assistant in an educational program.

Advanced Degrees in Child and Family Relations

There are advanced degrees in many associated child and family relations areas (social sciences, family and consumer sciences, and so on). The people who hold these degrees may go on to teach child care or family and consumer sciences in high school or a two-year college. You may also get an advanced degree to further your knowledge and performance in your work with children and families.

Master's programs are available for degrees in administration with special needs children or for individuals who desire to gain more knowledge and skills with curriculum, methods, materials, and teaching and learning styles of young children.

Child-Life Specialists

Academic preparation for the bachelor's degree at the child-life specialist level includes supervised experience in the health-care setting with competence in the following areas:[1]

- All forms of diversity
- Growth and development
- Family dynamics
- Play and activities
- Interpersonal communications
- Developmental observation and assessment
- The learning process
- The group process

---

1. "Child Life Services in Healthcare Settings." 2005. Child Life Council. www.childlife.org.

- Behavior management
- Reactions of children and family to illness or life-changing events
- Interventions to prevent emotional trauma
- Collaboration with other health professionals
- Basic understanding of children's illnesses and medical terminology
- Research supporting child-life practice
- Supervisory skills

Child-Life Assistant

A child-life assistant works under the direct supervision of a child-life specialist. Generally, a child-life assistant is a graduate from a two-year college in a related field and has personal qualifications similar to those of specialists. A year of teaching experience with children (infant through school age) in a group setting is preferred.

Related Degrees for Child-Life Careers

Several colleges have specific child-life undergraduate or graduate programs, but many universities have course work that is related to child-life degrees. (Contact the Child Life Council for a list of colleges and information.) Typical course work may include a broad range of standard liberal arts courses, such as English, history, science, and so on. A comprehensive major would also include courses relating to the healthy as well as the hospitalized child, such as the following:

Children under stress
Psychology of the exceptional child

Human growth and development
Psychosocial care of hospitalized children and adolescents

Field experiences in the junior or senior year are done in local hospitals, clinics, child care centers, preschools, and special education classes. A master's degree may be obtained with another one or two years of specialized study. A supervisory position is likely to be held by individuals with a graduate degree.

Requirements for Child-Life Careers

In the past, not all child-life specialists were necessarily graduates of these colleges. Individuals in related fields entered child-life positions because of previous work experience and on-the-job training programs. The basic skill of the child-life specialist is being able to handle the psychosocial needs of children in medical settings.

Since 1986 the Child Life Council has developed the Certified Child-Life Specialists (CCLS) credential to increase the proficiency of child-life professionals. To be eligible to take the Child Life Professional Certification Examination, of which successful completion earns the CCLS credential, you must first meet the following criteria:

1. Receive a baccalaureate degree, or be in the final semester of study toward a baccalaureate degree.
2. Complete ten college-level courses within the following areas: child life, child/family development, family dynamics, human development, psychology, sociology, counseling, education, expressive therapies, and therapeutic recreation.

3. Complete 480 hours of a child-life internship/fellowship or complete 480 hours of paid clinical child-life work experience. Either must be under the supervision of a certified child-life specialist.

To view documentation requirements, visit the Child Life Council's website at www.childlife.org/certification/eligibility_require ments%20.htm. According to this website, the benefits of certification for a child-life professional are:

Feelings of personal accomplishment and satisfaction
Validating specialized knowledge
Indicating professional growth
Attainment of a practice standard
Personal challenge
Professional commitment
Credibility
Possibility of increased salary

Contact the council for information on the most up-to-date child-life certification requirements:

Child Life Council
11820 Parklawn Drive, Suite 240
Rockville, MD 20852
www.childlife.org

Montessori Method

According to material provided by the American Montessori Society (AMS), there are different methods and ways to become a director or directress (teacher) in the Montessori system. The basics of the programs include the academic phase and the practicum phase.

A degree from a four-year accredited college is usually required for acceptance to the program. Although a background in child psychology or child development is desired, no specific field of study is required. There are different programs with the number of hours required varying in academic instruction and practicum phases. Between 300 and 350 hours of academic work are required in the concentrated academic phases.

Academic Phases

These will include study in historical and philosophical foundations of American education and relationships of Montessori principles to current theories of child development.

Montessori Specifics	*Methods Workshops*
Theory and philosophy	Practical life
Materials practicum	Sensorial
Observation	Mathematics
Montessori manual	Language arts
Child development/psychology	Creative arts
Studies (geography, music, and so on)	Science
	Social/environmental

Practicum Phase

The practicum phase uses both the theory and practice of Montessori education. This includes a nine-month teaching experience in an American Montessori Society–affiliated school. A course representative observes the student teacher. The student teacher serves as an observer and participant rather than taking on the responsibility of directing a class. There are two approved Montessori organizations: Association Montessori Internationale (AMI) and American Montessori Society (AMS). Contact these organizations for more information about different programs, schools, and requirements.

Association Montessori Internationale/USA
410 Alexander Street
Rochester, NY 14607-1028
http://ami.edu/usa

American Montessori Society, Inc.
281 Park Avenue South
New York, NY 10010-6102
www.amshq.org

Parent Educators

Parent educators, parent-child educators, family-life educators, family educators, or early childhood educators may have a license to teach parents or parent-child interaction as well as to plan and coordinate the instructional programs. As this is a state-licensed position, each state sets requirements. In working papers from the Minnesota Department of Education, here are two core areas and suggested courses for qualification. Contact your state certification office for your state's guidelines. Minnesota's licensing qualifications include the following:

1. A baccalaureate degree (B.S. or B.A.) from an accredited college or university
2. A parent educator core:

- Adult learning methods and materials
- Family development/family systems/family structure and function
- Parent education curriculum/methods and material
- Group facilitations/process/dynamics
- Parent-child relations
- Practicum or internship or experiences at the adult level

3. An early childhood teacher preparation program:

- Infant and toddler development
- Learning environments and modalities
- Parent-child relations
- Child development/child psychology
- Child health, nutrition, and safety
- Early childhood family education methods and materials
- Practicum, internship, or experience in early childhood family education

Parent educators work with parents. This degree is usually available as a vocational degree. Early childhood teacher degrees prepare a teacher to work with children. A combination degree such as early childhood family education gives the needed combination of knowledge of these two areas.

The field of parent educators is growing in preschool programs in which the teacher works with both the parents and the children. This combination degree qualifies you for this position without the need for two degrees (a vocational parent-educator degree and an early childhood teaching degree).

4

Related Careers

Child care is only one of many careers in which people work closely with children. People in a variety of specializations work directly with children but stress different aspects of caring for the social, psychological, intellectual, emotional, physical, and spiritual needs of children. People who are interested in direct work with children might want to explore careers in the following areas.

Teacher Assistants

Teacher assistants (also known as teacher aides, instructional aides, para-educators, and paraprofessionals) work in a wide variety of school settings. Nearly three in four work for state and local government education institutions.

A teacher assistant provides instructional and clerical support for classroom teachers. This allows the teacher to concentrate on direct teaching. An assistant may also supervise children on the playground, crossing streets, in nonteaching situations like in the cafeteria, or in the classroom. In 2002, 1.3 million jobs were held by teacher assistants—mostly in preschools and elementary schools.

In some school districts, an assistant may work directly with students under the supervision and guidance of a teacher and perform duties such as the following:

Supervise
Record grades
Set up equipment
Listen to children read
Work with groups
Work on special projects
Help students with computers

In other school districts, an assistant may only be allowed to do nonteaching duties such as the following:

Grading tests and papers
Checking homework
Keeping health and attendance records
Typing, filing, and duplicating material
Operating audiovisual equipment
Stocking supplies
Supervising nonclassroom activities

Working Conditions

More than half of the assistants work less than full-time. They may work indoors or outside. Much of the time may be spent standing, walking, or kneeling. Close work with students may be physically and emotionally draining.

Because children in special education are being integrated into general classrooms, many teacher assistants spend a lot of time assisting students with disabilities. Teacher assistants may also assist students with other special needs, such as those who speak English as a second (or other) language or those from disadvantaged families.

Training

Education requirements vary among schools. Some require high school diplomas, and others may require college training. Usually the more direct work with and teaching of children require more education. In many schools, previous experience working with children is also required.

Associate training (two-year programs) helps prepare students for assistant work. On-the-job training is also common for assistant preparation. Usually there will be a period of orientation to help assistants with:

Teaching handwriting, reading, math, science, and so on
Administering first aid
Operating audiovisual equipment
Keeping records
Making charts
Preparing bulletin boards

Personal Traits

Assistants must be able to relate to children and enjoy working with children from a wide range of cultural backgrounds. They must be able to be fair and patient in handling classroom situations. They must also be able to convey and follow teachers' instructions. Assistants must have basic writing and speaking skills in order to communicate with students and teachers. A talent for getting along with others is needed. Clerical skills may be needed along with organizational, cooperative, and record-keeping abilities.

Outlook

Employment is expected to increase somewhat faster than average through 2012. Teacher assistants are expected to work more in the high-demand areas of special education and special needs. The No Child Left Behind Act of 2001 has put a greater focus on educational quality and accountability in education, creating a greater demand for teacher assistants. Teachers will need more help preparing students for standardized tests. As in past years, teacher assistant positions are sensitive to budget cuts and constraints.

Earnings

In 2002 the median yearly earnings of teacher assistants were $18,660. The middle 50 percent earned between $14,880 and $23,050. The lowest 10 percent earned less than $12,900, and the highest 10 percent earned more than $29,050.

Sources for More Information

For more information, contact the following:

American Federation of Teachers, AFL-CIO
Paraprofessional and School Related Personnel Division
555 New Jersey Avenue NW
Washington, DC 20001
www.aft.org
(For information on teaching and certification)

National Education Association
Educational Support Personnel Division
1201 Sixteenth Street NW
Washington, DC 20036-3290
www.nea.org
(For information on teaching and certification)

National Resource Center for Paraprofessionals
Utah State University
6526 Old Main Hill
Logan, UT 84322-6526
www.nrcpara.org
(For career information on being a teacher assistant)

Health-Service Occupations

Health-service workers assist other professionals (physicians, dentists, optometrists, nurses, and therapists) in their duties. They perform routine, essential, and personal duties. They must converse with patients, make them feel comfortable, and set them at ease. They may work in institutions or with professionals who are specializing in children's health. Depending on where they work, their duties may be as follows:

Make appointments
Greet patients
Keep records
Deliver food trays
Change bed linens
Transport patients
Help patients do exercises
Escort patients who cannot walk unassisted

Nursing, psychiatric, and home health aides held two million jobs in 2002. They answer patient calls, deliver and collect food trays, feed patients, and relieve nursing staff of routine tasks.

Medical and dental assistants had 586,000 jobs in 2002. Usually they work in offices of practitioners and handle combination office and patient-care duties.

Working Conditions

Individuals in health-care careers have to help with the treatment of children who are sick, disabled, or infirm. They may move or assemble heavy equipment. They may also have to perform housekeeping chores.

In a hospital setting they may work fewer than forty hours per week; they may work nights, weekends, and holidays. Many long hours are spent standing. Duties will also include changing bedpans and bed linens. Personal satisfaction comes from helping those in need.

Training

Some individuals complete a one- to two-year program offered by community colleges or vocational or technical schools. Many jobs are entry-level positions that don't usually require previous work experience. A high school diploma is preferred, but it isn't always required. There are good opportunities for young adults as well as for middle-aged and older people seeking to reenter the labor force after family responsibilities change.

Many states require nursing aides to be certified by passing an approved course of instruction from a state-approved school. Courses from 65 to 240 hours are offered in high schools, community colleges, vocational or technical schools, and nursing care facilities.

Some states don't require certification, but aides are trained on the job after they are hired. Trainees take and record temperatures, bathe patients, change linens, and move and lift patients. Training may last a few days to a few months.

Personal Traits

Qualities needed for a person in health-related occupations are dependability, common sense, emotional stability, a cheerful disposition, and a willingness to assume responsibility. A fair amount of physical effort is needed, which at times is strenuous and tiring.

Outlook

Most employment in health services is expected to increase 28 percent through 2012, compared with 16 percent for all industries combined. This reflects anticipated demand for health-care services because of the growing population and longer life expectancy. This also reflects continued emphasis on using support personnel to increase productivity of highly trained practitioners.

Most job openings will come through the need to replace people in current positions. The number of job openings will continue to be numerous because of high turnover, minimal entry requirements, and low pay scale.

Earnings

Median hourly earnings of nursing aides, orderlies, and attendants were $9.59 in 2002. The middle 50 percent earned an hourly income between $8.06 and $11.39. The lowest 10 percent earned less than $6.98 an hour. The top 10 percent earned more than $13.54 an hour.

Median hourly earnings of home health aides were $8.70 in 2002. The middle 50 percent earned an hourly income between $7.54 and $10.37. The lowest 10 percent earned less than $6.56 an hour. The top 10 percent earned more than $12.34 an hour.

Median hourly earnings of psychiatric aides were $11.04 in 2002. The middle 50 percent earned an hourly income between $8.97 and $13.74 an hour. The lowest 10 percent earned less than $7.52. The top percent earned more than $16.16 an hour.

Median hourly earning of dental assistants were $13.10 in 2002. The middle 50 percent earned an hourly income between $10.35 and $16.20. The lowest 10 percent earned less than $8.45 an hour. The top 10 percent earned more than $19.41 an hour.

Median annual earnings of medical assistants were $23,940 in 2002. The middle 50 percent earned an annual income of $20,260 and $28,410. The lowest 10 percent earned less than $17,640. The top 10 percent earned more than $34,130.

Sources for More Information

Contact the following to find out more about your interests in health service occupations.

American Association of Medical Assistants
20 North Wacker Drive, Suite 1575
Chicago, IL 60606
www.aama-ntl.org
(For information about careers and educational programs in medical assisting)

American Dental Assistants Association
35 East Wacker Drive, Suite 1730
Chicago, IL 60601-2211
www.dentalassistant.org
(For information on dental assistant career opportunities)

American Dental Association
211 East Chicago Avenue
Chicago, IL 60611-2678
www.ada.org
(For information about accredited dental assistant programs)

American Society for Healthcare Human Resources Administration
One North Franklin
Chicago, IL 60606
www.ashhra.org
(For referrals to hospital human resource departments about local
   opportunities)

National Association for Home Care
228 Seventh Street SE
Washington, DC 20003
www.nahc.org
(For information on the training and certification of home health
   aides)

Licensed Practical/Vocational Nurses

A licensed practical nurse (L.P.N.) helps care for physically or mentally ill people under the direction of a physician and registered nurse (R.N.). An L.P.N may specialize in the care of children. Duties may include the following:

Bedside care

Taking and recording temperatures and blood pressure

Changing dressings

Administering prescribed medications .

Helping patients with bathing, brushing teeth, and other
  personal hygiene

Assisting doctors and R.N.s in examining patients

Carrying out nursing procedures

Assisting in the delivery, care, and feeding of infants

In private homes, L.P.N.s may offer nursing care, prepare meals, see to patient comfort, keep up morale, or teach other family members to perform simple nursing tasks.

Working Conditions

An L.P.N. may work a forty-hour week that could also include some night, weekend, and holiday work. They must stand for long periods of time. They must be able to help patients move in bed, stand, and walk.

In private homes, the L.P.N. may work eight to twelve hours a day and go home at night. The L.P.N. will have much more independence in setting work hours and length and frequency of vacations in a private setting.

In 2002 there were 702,000 L.P.N. positions. About 28 percent of these jobs were found in hospitals, 26 percent in nursing care facilities, and another 12 percent in offices of physicians. Other jobs were found in educational services, community-care facilities, outpatient-care centers, and government agencies. Approximately one out of five L.P.N.s worked part-time.

Training

L.P.N.s are required to have a license. They must complete a state-approved program in practical nursing. A high school diploma or its equivalent usually is required to enter the practical nursing courses. Training lasts one year and includes both classroom study and clinical practice. In 2002 training in practical nursing was available in eleven hundred state-approved programs.

Personal Traits

L.P.N.s must have a deep regard for human welfare and be emotionally stable, as work with sick and injured children can be upsetting. The L.P.N. must be able to follow orders as part of a health team and work under close supervision.

Outlook

Employment for L.P.N.s is expected to rise about as fast as the average through the year 2012. Positions filled will be mostly through replacement. Opportunities should be excellent in nursing-care facilities and home health-care services.

Earnings

A full-time L.P.N.'s annual median wage in 2002 was $31,440. The range was from under $22,860 to $44,040 per year.

Sources for More Information

Contact the following to find out more about opportunities working as an L.P.N.

National Association for Practical Nurse Education
and Services, Inc.
P.O. Box 25647
Alexandria, VA 22313
www.napnes.org
(For information on education and certification)

National Federation of Licensed Practical Nurses, Inc.
605 Poole Drive
Garner, NC 27529
www.nflpn.org
(For information about careers in practical nursing)

National League for Nursing
61 Broadway
New York, NY 10006
www.nln.org
(For a list of state-approved training programs and information
about practical nursing)

Social Worker

Social workers are people-oriented professionals who use a variety
of techniques to help individuals and families whose lives are being
torn apart by poverty, alcoholism, drug abuse, behavioral problems,
or illness.

They find families to adopt or provide foster care for children
whose parents are unable to take care of them. They also see that
needy families are able to give their children proper food, health
care, and schooling. Social workers step in where parents neglect or
abuse children. Specialties may be as follows:

Child, family, and school social worker
Medical and public health social worker
Mental health and substance abuse social worker
Occupational social worker

Working Conditions

Usually a social worker works a standard forty-hour week. Those at many private agencies work part-time. Many work evenings and weekends to meet clients, attend community meetings, and handle emergency situations. Some travel is required as social workers attend meetings and visit clients.

Training

A bachelor's degree in psychology, sociology, or social work is a minimum requirement. A master's degree in social work (M.S.W.) is required for mental health, supervisory, administrative, or research positions. A doctorate is required for teaching and is desirable for some research and administrative jobs.

Personal Traits

Social workers must be emotionally mature, objective, and sensitive. They must possess a basic concern for people and their problems and be able to handle responsibilities, work independently, and maintain good working relationships with clients and coworkers.

Outlook

Employment in social work is expected to increase faster than average through 2012. Most positions will come from replacing those who quit or leave their jobs. Expansion is likely in hospices, nursing homes, and long-term care facilities. Social workers held about 477,000 jobs in 2002.

Earnings

Earnings vary according to the setting and degrees held by social workers. In January 2002, child, family, and school social workers averaged $33,150 per year. Social workers in medical and public health specialties averaged $37,380 in 2002. Mental health and substance abuse social workers on average earned $32,850 in 2002.

Sources for More Information

Contact the following to find out more about opportunities in social work.

Council on Social Work Education
1725 Duke Street, Suite 500
Alexandria, VA 22314-3457
www.cswe.org
(For a listing of accredited social work programs)

National Association of Social Workers
750 First Street NE, Suite 700
Washington, DC 20002-4241
www.socialworkers.org
(For information about career opportunities in social work)

Recreation and Fitness Worker

Recreation workers plan, organize, and direct activities to help people enjoy and benefit from leisure hours. Many recreation workers deal with children. They may work in a variety of settings such as the following:

Local playgrounds and community centers
Parks and tourist attractions
Campgrounds and recreational areas
Schools and churches

They may organize and conduct a variety of activities in arts and crafts, camping, fitness, or sports.

Working Conditions

Recreation workers may work forty hours a week with some night and weekend work, irregular hours, and much time spent outdoors. Most jobs are in urban and suburban areas, but jobs are also found in camping areas.

Recreation and fitness workers held approximately 485,000 jobs in 2002. Over 62 percent were recreation workers; the rest were fitness trainers and aerobic instructors. Almost 40 percent of the recreation workers with year-round jobs were in local government, such as in park and recreation departments. Fourteen percent were in membership organizations such as Boy Scouts, Girl Scouts, and Red Cross groups. Another 12 percent of recreation workers were in nursing and other personal care facilities. Many jobs are filled part-time by teachers and college students in the following areas:

Summer camp counselors
Lifeguards
Craft specialists
Leadership and recreational programs

Training

Training for recreation and fitness workers varies greatly with the job. Many college graduates have degrees in recreation, leisure, health, fitness, exercise science, or physical education. But other degreed individuals and some high school graduates also may fill positions. Most supervisors have a bachelor's degree plus experience. A bachelor's degree and experience are minimal requirements for administration.

Personal Traits

A recreation or fitness worker must have the following traits:

Be good at motivating people
Be sensitive to people's needs
Be healthy
Have physical stamina
Be creative
Be resourceful
Accept responsibility
Exercise judgment
Be able to work alone

Outlook

Employment for recreation and fitness workers is expected to increase faster than the average through the year 2012. Opportunities in fitness careers are expected to rise due to the growing interest in fitness activities. Competition will be high, and those individuals with recreation experience and formal training have the best opportunities.

Earnings

Median hourly earnings of recreation workers who worked full-time in 2002 were about $8.69. The middle 50 percent earned between $7.09 and $11.36. The top 10 percent earned $15.72 or more.

Median hourly earnings of fitness trainers and aerobics instructors in 2002 were $11.51. The middle 50 percent earned between $8.06 and $18.18. The top 10 percent earned $26.22 or more.

Sources for More Information

Contact the following to find out more about your interests in recreation and fitness.

American Camping Association
5000 State Road 67 North
Martinsville, IN 46151-7902
www.acacamps.org
(For information about careers as camp counselors)

American Council on Exercise
4851 Paramount Drive
San Diego, CA 92123
www.acefitness.org
(For information on careers and certification in the fitness field)

National Recreation and Park Association
Division of Professional Services
22377 Belmont Ridge Road
Ashburn, VA 20148-4501
www.nrpa.org
(For information on careers, certification, and academic programs
    in parks and recreation)

Psychologist

Applied psychologists counsel patients and conduct training programs, do market research, and provide health services in hospitals and clinics. Some specialized psychologists work with children. For example, a child psychologist deals with behavior during infancy and childhood. A clinical psychologist works in a hospital or in a private practice in a clinic. Psychologists help clients with mental or emotional problems adjust to life. A school psychologist evaluates students' needs and problems.

Working Conditions

Specialty and place of employment will determine a psychologist's working conditions. Many experience pressures of deadlines because of the following factors:

Tight schedules
Heavy workload
Overtime work
Frequent interruptions of routine
Travel to conferences or research

About 139,000 psychologists were employed in 2002. Medical settings employed 30 percent of psychologists. Educational settings employed 30 percent. Government agencies at the state and local levels employed 10 percent. Over 25 percent were self-employed.

Training

A doctorate degree is often required for people entering this occupation. A person with a master's degree may administer tests as an assistant. They may counsel patients, perform administrative duties, teach in a two-year college, or work as a school psychologist or as an industrial-organizational psychologist.

Those with a bachelor's degree may assist psychologists and other professionals in mental health settings, vocational rehabilitation, correctional programs, or in government or business as trainees. They also may teach high school if they meet state requirements.

Personal Traits

Psychologists have to be emotionally stable, mature, and able to deal with people effectively. It is also important to be sensitive, compassionate, and able to lead and inspire others. Results may take a long time, so patience and perseverance are also desired traits.

Outlook

Because of their high investment in training, psychologists have a strong attachment to the field—only a few leave each year. Employment is expected to increase faster than average through the year 2012. Most jobs come from job replacement.

Ph.D. holders from leading universities should have good job prospects in clinical, counseling, health, and industry areas. Those with quantitative research methods and computer science backgrounds will have an edge over those without. People with master's degrees will have severe competition for limited jobs. Those with bachelor's degrees have very few opportunities. Some might find jobs as assistants in rehabilitation centers.

Earnings

In 2002, median annual earnings of clinical, counseling, and school psychologists were $51,170. The middle 50 percent earned between

$38,560 and $66,970. The top 10 percent earned more than $87,060.

Median earnings of industrial-organizational psychologists were $63,710 per year. The middle 50 percent earned between $48,540 and $81,880. The top 10 percent earned more than $112,660 per year.

Sources for More Information

Contact the following associations to find out more about opportunities in psychology.

American Board of Professional Psychology, Inc.
514 East Capitol Avenue
Jefferson City, MO 65101
www.abpp.org
(For information about psychology specialty certifications)

American Psychological Association
750 First Street NE
Washington, DC 20002
www.apa.org
(For information on careers, education requirements, and financial
    assistance in all fields of psychology)

National Association of School Psychologists
4340 East West Highway, Suite 401
Bethesda, MD 20814
www.nasponline.org
(For information on careers, education requirements, and
    certification in school psychology)

Other Related Careers

Other positions work directly with children but specialize in specific areas. The areas and degrees of specialization are limitless, but include:

Children's librarian, assistant, and aide
Family and children's counselor/therapist
Youth pastor
Children's unit R.N.
Special education
Obstetrical R.N.
Child psychiatrist
Pediatrician

There is also a wide range of specialties, such as dance, drama, singing, teaching instruments, swimming, crafts, and others that may fall into recreational or teaching careers that include direct work with children.

5

Reaching Goals in Education and Employment

You know what the job duties are, where the jobs are located, and what qualifications you need. Now, how do you get the job? You might be lucky and get a good work experience or practicum in the kind of place you want to work. Your supervisors are impressed with you and your work. There happens to be an opening, and they offer you the job. That does happen, but not very often. So how should you go about looking for a job?

Self-Evaluation

As you prepare to enter the world of work, first ask yourself some questions and make some lists. What things do I like doing? What things do I dislike doing? What kind of job do I see myself working in? What is important to me? Consider the following:

Working with my hands	Money
Respect	Status
Need space	Doing a job well
Close contact with people	Teaching
Adults to look up to me	Children to look up to me
Need time to myself	Like order
Reaching goals	Like neatness
Working with people	Working independently
Being a good worker	Being a supervisor
Patience	Being spontaneous
Planning ahead	Being part of a group

Other questions to think about include the following:

Does this career help me do and accomplish what I want?
What are my qualifications—skills, experience, training?
What qualifications are needed for my ideal job?
What am I lacking now?
What can I change?
What can't I change?
Is my job goal realistic?

Goal Evaluation

Before you get into evaluating your goal, you have to know what your goal is. Write down exactly what your ultimate goal is. For example, you may write "nursery school teacher." Next make a list of things that need to be accomplished or answered for you to reach your goal. For example:

Am I Qualified?
Find out your state's requirements.
Determine if you need more education or training.
Find out if there are alternative ways to qualify.

Do I Really Want This Job?
Interview a nursery or preschool teacher.
Visit a nursery or preschool.
Volunteer or work as a substitute for experience.
Request information from the library.
Contact related organizations and associations.
Talk to your high school or career counselor.
Talk to your state employment counselor.

If I Need More Education or Training, How Do I Get It?
Get a list of recommended schools.
Check into alternative training such as on-the-job training.
Check into funding for training programs.
Choose a school and contact it for information.
Check into work-study programs available through schools
    or at work sites.

How Far Am I Willing to Look to Get the Job?
Only in my city—check the yellow pages and schools and
    friends.
Within driving distance—also check with chamber of
    commerce offices and community bulletin boards.
Statewide—check with state associations, job services, and
    the others already listed.

Anywhere—also check for other states' qualifications, national organizations, and school placement offices.

Financial Aid

Financial aid can help many families meet college costs. Almost one-half of all students who go on for more education after high school receive financial aid of some kind. There are three main types of financial assistance that are available to qualified students at the college level: grants and scholarships, loans, and work-study programs.[1]

Grants and scholarships provide aid that does not have to be paid back. However, some require that recipients maintain certain grade levels or take certain courses.

Loans are another type of financial aid and are available to both students and parents. A loan eventually must be repaid. Often payments do not begin until the student finishes school, and the interest rate on education loans is usually lower than for other types of loans.

Work-study programs are also ways to get money for college. Many students work during the summer and/or part-time during the school year to help pay for college. Although many students obtain jobs on their own, many colleges also offer work-study programs to their students. A work-study job is often part of a student's financial aid package. The jobs are usually on campus, and the money earned is used to pay for tuition or other college charges.

---

1. U.S. Department of Education. *The Student Guide: Financial Aid from the U.S. Department of Education*, 2005–2006 edition, on the Internet at http://studentaid.ed.gov/students/attachments/siteresources/Stud_guide.pdf.

The types of financial aid discussed above can be based on merit, need, or a combination. Merit-based financial aid is usually given to students who meet requirements not related to financial needs. For example, a merit scholarship may be given to a student who has done well in high school or who displays artistic or athletic talent. Most merit-based aid is awarded on the basis of academic performance or potential. Need-based financial aid means that the amount of aid a student can receive depends on the cost of the college and on his or her family's ability to pay these costs. Most financial aid is need-based and is available to qualified students.

Students can receive financial aid through a number of sources, including the federal government, state governments, colleges and universities, and other organizations. Students can receive aid from more than one source.

Federal Financial Assistance

The federal government supplies the largest amount of all student aid. Applying for federal student aid is free. Simply fill out the Free Application for Federal Student Aid (FAFSA). The FAFSA is available online; visit www.fafsa.ed.gov. The largest and most popular federal student aid programs include Federal Pell Grants, which are need-based grants. In the 2004–5 school year, the maximum Pell Grant was $4,050. Also, since 1992, Federal Stafford Loans have been offered under two programs: one need based (subsidized) and the other non-need based (nonsubsidized). Under the need-based program, the federal government pays the interest on the loan while the student is in school, and the student starts paying back the loan and the interest after graduation. Under the non-need-based program, the interest accrues while the student is in school. After graduation, the student must pay back both the loan and the interest on the loan, including the interest that accrued while the student was in school.

The federal government also provides money to colleges to give to needy students. There are three campus-based programs: a grant program (Federal Supplemental Educational Opportunity Grants or FSEOGs), a loan program (Federal Perkins Loans), and the Federal Work-Study Program. For up-to-date information on student aid supplied by the federal government, call the Federal Student Financial Aid Information Center toll-free at the U.S. Department of Education, 1-800-4FED-AID or visit www.studentaid.ed.gov. You can also access *The Student Guide* online, which provides an extensive and updated discussion of all federal student aid programs. Go to: http://studentaid.ed.gov/students/publications/student_guide/index.htm.

Other Financial Assistance

Some states offer either need- or merit-based financial assistance directly to students. To find out about state aid where you live, call or write your state's higher education agency.

Other types of aid may be offered directly from the colleges themselves. Most of this "institutional aid" is in the form of scholarships or grants. Some is based on need and some on merit. Contact the financial aid offices of the schools that you are considering attending to request information.

In addition, many specific organizations offer financial help. Some books available in libraries that may help you find private sources of financial aid include: *Foundation Grants to Individuals*, fourteenth edition, The Foundation Center, 2005; *The A's and B's of Academic Scholarships: 100,000 Scholarships for Top Students*, twenty-fifth edition, Anna Leider, Octameron Associates; 2005; and *The Scholarship Book: The Complete Guide to Private-Sector Scholarships, Fellowships, Grants, and Loans for the Undergraduate*, twelfth edition, National Scholarship Research Service, Prentice Hall Press, 2006.

College admissions offices and high school guidance counselors should also be able to provide more information about scholarships.

Job Listings

Once you have prepared yourself with all the experience, information, and education you need, you are ready to apply for the job. Some places to check for listings of jobs are child care magazines, professional journals, and perhaps even civil service announcements (check at the state employment or job service office). If you don't have a specific place in mind, but you know what town or city you want to work in, try the yellow pages, the city's website, or the chamber of commerce offices to find listings of child care centers, schools, hospitals, or other work sites. The Internet is also a valuable source for job listings. There are countless websites dedicated to posting available jobs. America's Job Bank is a great place to start your search; visit www.ajb.dni.us.

Some organizations and associations also offer job banks or job listings to their members:

- The Child Life Council offers a job bank for its members (www.childlife.org).
- The National Coalition for Campus Children's Centers publishes a directory of NCCCC members yearly and offers

an e-mail ListServ. This might be a source for on-campus jobs (www.campuschildren.org).

- A directory of nanny placement agencies can be found on the International Nanny Association's website (www.nanny.org).

Other organizations, associations, or groups may advertise child care positions in their newsletters, journals, or websites.

Résumé

Before you start applying for positions, create a résumé. A résumé is usually a one-sheet typed paper that describes who you are, how to reach you, what your background and experience are, and what kind of job you want.

A résumé is important because it will represent you to the employer. By creating a résumé ahead of time, you will also have a lot of information about your education, work history, skills, and accomplishments at your fingertips and in front of an employer before you even fill out an application.

How do you write one? What do you stress? That depends on you. Do you have schooling in child care development or education? Do you have experience? Are your babysitting skills and ability to get along with young children your strong points? Place the information in the order of importance to the job. List your strong points first.

Here is an example of things to include in a résumé:

Personal Information
Name (your first and last name)
Address (an address where you want mail to be sent)
Phone number (your home or mobile phone number)

E-mail address (an e-mail address that you check often)
Position applying for (title of position)

Education
List most recent education first.
List degree, school, address, date graduated.

Work Experiences
List any work experiences and dates and the names and addresses of your employers. Then describe your job duties. The following list will give you some ideas.

Practicums
Field experiences
Internships
Part-time and full-time jobs
Volunteer experiences
Babysitting jobs
Child care or preschool experiences

Related Experiences
List any related skills and experiences, including:

Hobbies
Special talents or skills
Any experience with children
Experience teaching or playing an instrument
Arts and crafts
Experience with children's clubs
Experience teaching religious school
Experience setting up a play group

Other Attributes
Relate well to children
Enjoy arts and crafts with children
Enjoy music
Patient
Organized

You should also list at least three good references on your résumé. Try to list people who have seen you working with children or who can vouch for your character. Don't use relatives. Employers, teachers, clergy, and parents of children you have cared for are especially good references. Give their names, addresses, occupations, and phone numbers.

If you don't have relevant education, you should still list your high school and other college or vocational training. But instead of listing education first, put it farther down on the page. If your work history is more important, then list that right after the personal data. If you don't have related education or work history, find your strong points and factually list or describe them first (after your name, address, and so on).

Talk to the people that you plan to use as references. Ask them if they believe they could recommend you for the position for which you are applying. Ask for their permission to use their names as references. In child care positions your references are likely to be checked out. Choose people who know you personally, who have worked with you, or who have supervised you. You need someone who can vouch for your character as well as your work habits.

What kinds of questions might an employer ask about you? Here are some common questions. As you read through them, be honest and answer them about yourself. As you answer the questions, consider what areas you may need to work on.

Is the applicant trustworthy and honest?
Is the applicant reliable by coming to school or work every
    day and on time?
Does the applicant finish tasks?
How does the applicant relate to children?
How do children relate to the applicant?
How are problems handled?
What is the applicant's temperament?
How does the applicant get along with supervisors, parents,
    coworkers, or friends?
Is the applicant easy to talk or work with?
What are the applicant's good or strong points?
What are the applicant's bad or weak points?
How does the applicant handle stress or a crisis?

In addition to your listed references, the employer might check coworkers, supervisors, and parents of children with whom you have worked.

Looking for the Jobs

Word of mouth is a common way of finding out about jobs. If a position is going to be open, centers or schools might list the opening on their bulletin boards, tell parents through a newsletter, list openings in community agencies, run an ad in the newspaper, list with employment offices, post jobs online, or go to their on-file applications. Other professional positions might be listed through organizations and associations or job banks.

If you know where you want to work, phone to see if any positions are available or might become available soon. Ask if they keep active applications on file. If there is an opening or if they keep active applications, express an interest. Ask when would be a good time for you to stop by and fill out an application.

You could just stop by, but you are apt to make a better impression if you let them suggest a time for you to come when it isn't so hectic. You then might have an opportunity to visit and observe while you are there. You may be able to get an "informal" interview even if there isn't an opening—yet.

Application Form

Before interviewing, if there are a lot of applicants, people are going to be screened—chosen for interviews or eliminated as a possibility—on the basis of the application. Read and follow directions on the application carefully. If it says print in ink, don't write cursive in pencil. Be complete and neat; answer questions briefly but as completely as possible. Have all information with you. An application may include the following:

Name, mailing address, phone number, e-mail address
Driver's license number
Present job—reasons for wanting to leave, salary
Past employment—reasons for leaving, salaries
Special skills
Other accomplishments
References

Many of these items will be listed on your résumé or personal data sheet, but complete the application as directed.

If you have young children, you might be asked whether you plan to have the children attend where you work. This is not always encouraged. Find out ahead of time what the policy is on that issue. Be able to respond to questions about your own children's care and health. These might not really be legitimate questions, but they might come up in personal conversations if not during the actual interview.

Unfortunately, some employers in the child care field aren't any more sympathetic or understanding about your child care problems at home than any other employer (although many are). Child care work sites need reliable caregivers. By law they need one adult for a certain number of children. If the caregiver or teacher is unreliable, then so are their services. This is one good reason to see if they have substitutes available.

Interview

After sorting through applications, the best applicants are chosen to come in for interviews. If you are called, remember some very basic things:

Be clean   use good personal hygiene.
Don't smoke or chew gum.
Dress in clean, neat clothing. (Dress slightly better than
    you would for work.)
Be on time (if not a bit early).
Come alone. (If you have children, leave them with friends
    or relatives.)

The questions asked might help the employer determine how you feel and think about many different subjects. Listen carefully to the questions and answer them as seriously and honestly as possible. Besides your attitude, the interviewer will question you about your skills and abilities.

Some questions may address some of your personal likes and dislikes. Your responses will be documented and later ranked against other applicants. In addition to noting your answers, the interviewer will also be making notes on other personal observations. How you act and dress and your personality will count. Some questions that you might be asked are as follows:

Why are you applying for this job?
What do you think you can add to this child care center, school, or institution?
What part of this work do you enjoy the most?
What part of this work do you enjoy the least?
What kind of related work experiences do you have?
What are your career goals?
What are your weak points?
How do you feel about taking additional training/classes?

Selection

After all the interviews are completed, the interviewer or a committee or council will choose several finalists. When the choice is narrowed to one or two applicants, these final checks are performed:

Verification of application facts
Checking references

Checking for prior convictions for child abuse or child
    sexual abuse
Possibly some fingerprinting
Review of all data (résumé, application, interview)

One final step may be taken. The employer may wish to observe
you in an actual work situation. If you are presently working, an
observation may be made there. More likely, however, you will be
asked to come to your new work site for a final interview and to
spend some time with the children. However, the smaller the work
site and the fewer applicants, the more informal the interview process might be.

Your Decision

If you have any unanswered questions, be sure to get answers before
the end of the final interview. You are applying for the job. If you
are offered the job, the final step is still up to you to accept it or not.
    Ask yourself these questions, keeping in mind your goals.

Where does this job fit in?
Do you plan to get additional training, experience, or
    education to make you more qualified for promotions?
What do you want from the job? (Is it a position you
    wanted or is it only a stepping-stone?)
What will this position offer you?

Be sure to also get questions about the job and personnel policy
answered before you make up your mind. You may want consider
asking about the following:

What is the job description?
Is there a personnel policy that you can see?
Is there a performance appraisal system?
What is the beginning salary and the salary range?
Are there any career-advancement opportunities?
What, if any, are the fringe benefits: vacation or sick leave,
    health, life, and other insurance?
Is there a probationary period?

Once you have your answers, you will be better prepared to make an informed decision about your career.

6

CHANGES IN THE FIELD OF CHILD CARE

WHAT CAN YOU expect from the field of child care? Change. To quote a favorite expression, "Change is not made without inconvenience, even from worse to better." Stricter standards are being applied to provide protection and better services to children. Higher educational requirements are being placed on eligibility for jobs. People working in some jobs might find themselves ineligible for their current position, or they might move from professional to supportive staff. It is true, though, that some people may be "grandfathered" in. That means that if a person is in a position when new regulations come into effect, he or she would retain that position. However, this is by no means the rule. The emphasis is on education, professionalism, and improving the field of child care. This is change. It is good. It is inconvenient.

Advantages

The reward of choosing a child care career comes largely in the sense of fulfillment and satisfaction. It is being a part of the children's development and growth. You won't find the work boring or mundane. Your work may be very creative and individualized, depending upon your own talents and interests. You will learn and your knowledge will grow as you work with children. Rewards are also found in the closeness and bonds with other parents and professionals in the field.

The Educational Resource Information Center (ERIC) on Elementary and Early Childhood Education (EECE) did a Short Report-4 on *Staff "Burnout" in Child Care Settings*. It listed three main areas that pleased child care workers the most:

- Direct work with children
- Opportunity to learn and develop personal skills while working
- The fact that no two days are alike

The need for child care is increasing in all fields. Mothers of children who are preschool aged are again entering the labor force in increasing numbers. According to the Bureau of Labor Statistics, the demand for child care workers in general is expected to increase about as fast as average for all child care occupations through the year 2012, whereas the projected growth for the child day-care services industry alone is 43 percent. This faster-than-average employment growth paired with high replacement needs should create numerous employment opportunities.

In addition to the expected increase in the number of children under the age of five receiving care between 2002 and 2012, the proportion of youngsters in child care and preschool is expected to increase, reflecting a shift in type of child care arrangements for a variety of reasons. Parents may need two incomes to support a certain standard of living; they may find it too difficult to set up a satisfactory arrangement with a relative, babysitter, or live-in worker; or they may prefer the formal arrangements for personal reasons, such as a more structured learning environment.

Rising labor force participation among mothers ages fifteen to forty-four will also contribute to the growth of employment for child care workers. Today women with young children are as likely to work as other women, and more mothers are returning to work sooner after childbirth. Changes in perceptions of early childhood education may also lead more parents to seek child care for their children. Parents working weekends, evenings, and late nights will increase the demand for child care programs with nontraditional hours. If states start implementing mandatory preschool for four-year-old children, then the demand for preschool teachers will also grow. Greater employer involvement in funding and operating child care centers as a benefit to their employees could also lead to more children being cared for in centers. All of these factors will contribute to the continued increase in the need for child care workers.

Working Parents and Their Children

The 2004 American Community Survey lists the percentage of children under the age of six with both parents in the labor force at 59.5 percent. Households with children under the age of eighteen with both parents in the labor force reached approximately 44.8 million. These children have to be taken care of by somebody.

The availability of jobs in child care will be affected by the programs offered, the costs of care, and the supplemental assistance given to parents or to the programs to make child care affordable. The need for child care is great, and it would be used to an even greater extent if child care services were provided at an affordable cost and were accessible to everyone who needed it. With 18.1 percent of families with children under the age of eighteen being at poverty level in 2004, according to the U.S. Census Bureau, some parents simply cannot afford child care without some form of government assistance.

Disadvantages

Although standards are rising and with them some wages are being pulled up, low pay is still associated with this occupation. Being referred to as *babysitters* and having few adults to talk to during child-centered workdays contribute to low self-esteem. At times long hours are also required. Benefits, such as vacation time, sick leave, medical insurance, and health and life insurance vary among jobs, and they range from fair to nonexistent. Most employers in this field do offer free or discounted child care to employees. About half of child care workers have health benefits, and fewer than 20 percent have a retirement plan.

In its 2004 compendium, *Current Data on the Salaries and Benefits of the U.S. Early Childhood Education Workforce*, the Center for the Childcare Workforce states that the quality of care and education that children receive is directly affected by the working conditions and the education/training levels of those adults who are responsible for the children's care and education. Low pay, lack of benefits, and high staff turnover are, unfortunately, still realities of the child care field, but higher expectations are growing.

A National Early Care and Education Focus

More attention is being given to early childhood care and education and to improving the educational standards and working conditions of the workers themselves. The No Child Left Behind Act has put greater demands on schools (administrators, principals, teachers, and so forth) to demonstrate academic success of their students as early as third grade, which in turn shifts attention to the children's prekindergarten years and the importance of early learning and preparation. Because of this new focus, many states are developing and implementing state-funded prekindergarten programs. More focus is also being put on developing more training and professional development programs for child care providers. These programs are often linked to financial rewards to give workers greater incentive. Even though this progression toward improving early education for both the children and the providers is being observed, the progress is slow moving.

Growing Concerns

There are other areas that cause problems for child care providers. They are not related directly to the teaching or caregiver duties but to regulations that affect them. A change in laws or policies can do away with or accentuate their impact on child care workers.

Insurance and Child Care Liability

Stemming initially from reports of child abuse in child care centers, insurance and liability became issues. Child care providers can be sued and therefore need protection. Child care workers often need to make difficult decisions regarding the children they care for. Whether adequate care was taken in making those decisions can be the subject of a lawsuit. These decisions can include issues concerning policies as well as day-to-day supervision.

A publication of the Women's Bureau of the U.S. Department of Labor, *Child Care Liability and Insurance Primer*, says to reduce risk by simply keeping in mind that actions in making decisions and supervising the children that can lead to lawsuits will often lead to a course of action that eliminates hazards and improves the quality of care. Also, be sure that all local and state codes are complied with. Child care resource and referral networks may have further suggestions about risk control or may have references to safety consultants. Insurance companies, private attorneys, bar associations, and state and local agencies may also have resources in this regard.

In 1985 there was a shortage of child care insurance coverage. Today liability insurance is considered a necessity in the field of child care, and it is available through your choice of insurance provider. Some organizations like the Redleaf National Institute offer helpful articles such as "How to Pick a Business Liability Insurance Policy," "Just What Is Adequate Liability Coverage," and "Choosing a Liability Insurance Provider," among others. To look for affordable insurance coverage, locate an insurance broker or agent who has developed some familiarity with child care insurance or who is willing to spend the time necessary to become familiar with it. The Redleaf National Institute provides a list of liability insurance providers on its website at www.redleafinstitute.org. Also, consult with other providers in the area. Other sources may include national child care organizations, child care consultants, or the state insurance commissioner.

Facility Standards

In some states standards for family home child care were raised to be compatible with child care center standards. This caused many family child care homes to close down or operate unlicensed or without approval. Many of the fire, safety, and health codes necessary for centers are inappropriate or uncommon for a typical family dwelling.

For example, in Minnesota many family child care homes use the basement for indoor play. At first all you needed were windows large enough to help the children through in case of a fire. But regulations changed to insist on having an outside door leading from the basement. This was fine for older homes with basement steps leading to the outside and for newer split-level walkout homes, but many homes had no such openings.

Impact of Information

According to ERIC/EECE there is a common assumption in society that child care is an occupation that requires few skills. As long as child care work is considered unskilled, its low pay and status will reflect this viewpoint. Education of the general public and the upgrading of the child care professional are making a big impact on these misconceptions.

The more the public knows about child development and the impact of good programs, the higher status child care workers will enjoy. The movement today shows this:

- Parent/family educators have increased in numbers.
- Child care givers/providers have become more professional.

- Early education programs are not only offered but encouraged for children as young as newborns. Many states even offer state-funded prekindergarten programs.
- Pre-parenting classes are being developed and offered in some high schools, community centers, and colleges.
- More education and training is being required for workers in all areas of caregiving, education, and special needs.

Corporate Support

After its initial push, industry-supported child care ceased to develop as quickly as originally expected. In 1990 only 11 percent of all employers offered direct child care benefits. Most of the benefits were to full-time working women with higher educations and salaries. With an increase of couples and single parents in the labor force, there came a greater need for inexpensive and convenient child care. Refer to the Table 6.1 for percentages of the child care benefits that companies offered in the early 2000s depending on the number of employees.

According to the U.S. Department of Labor, women are projected to make up approximately 47 percent of the labor force in 2012. They will also account for 55 percent of the total growth in the labor force from 2002 to 2012. With a shrinking labor pool and a thriving service sector economy, women's employment needs have become even more important. Men, too, feel the problems of combining work and family life, as more than half of working men have wives who also work full- or part-time. Employers are being forced to respond to employees' needs to balance work and family responsibilities.

Table 6.1 Employer Work/Life Programs Vary by Company Size (Percentage of Companies Offering the Program)

Employer Program	*Number of Company Employees*			
	under 100	*100–250*	*250–999*	*1,000+*
On-site services	9%	7%	5%	18%
Child care center	4%	3%	3%	8%
Backup child care	5%	4%	5%	9%
Child care resource and referral (CCR&R)	36%	24%	39%	50%
Broad child care supports				
Community contribution	9%	6%	9%	13%
Public/private projects	11%	16%	7%	9%

Source: National Child Care Information Center (NCCIC). "Employer-Supported Child Care," 2004. On the Internet at www.nccic.org/poptopics/employersupportedcc.pdf.

The Family and Medical Leave Act of 1993

The Family and Medical Leave Act of 1993 was signed into law on February 5, 1993. It provides the American worker with the right to take unpaid, job-protected leave for meeting family health needs as well as for the worker's own illness. Women's organizations and family-rights supporters were encouraged by this act and transferred their attentions to child care issues. These groups proposed legislation that would compel all companies to provide some form of child care assistance. Other ideas were to restructure corporate tax incentives to allow lower-paid employees to receive child care benefits. They also called for allocations of federal funds for training of more infant-care workers. Direct financing for child care from state and federal governments was also suggested.

According to the Employment Policy Foundation's report, *The American Workplace 2005: The Changing Nature of Employee Benefits*, 32 percent of employers provided some form of child care assistance for their employees in 2004. Most companies accomplish this by providing a dependent care information service and/or financial assistance. The main forms of assistance are as follows:[1]

On-site or near-site child care centers
Consortium centers (partnering with other employers)
Resource and referral for child care
Vouchers
Discounts
Programs for part-time or emergency care
Sick-child care
Dependent care spending assistance plan (DCAP)
Odd-hour care

On-Site or Near-Site Child Care Centers

In 2001 approximately 9 percent of all companies provided financial support for or sponsored child care centers on or near the work site. Many employers subsidized the cost. Liability insurance is usually available at reasonable rates.

Consortium Centers (Partnering with Other Employers)

Consortium centers are when groups of employers share the cost and benefits of establishing and operating a child care center. This

---

1. U.S. Department of Labor, Women's Bureau. "Work and Family Resource Kit: Dependent Care Options." Washington, DC: U.S. Department of Labor, 1992.

is advantageous to small employers who cannot afford to operate such centers by themselves. Consortia are popular in industrial parks, shopping malls, and downtown locations. It is often best to have a neutral coordinator in a consortium effort. Resources, liability, and costs are shared, but such an arrangement also calls for cooperation among companies.

Resource and Referral for Child Care

Resource and referral services counsel employees on how to find and judge quality child care. They improve the quality of care by providing training for child care providers. An effective referral program increases the supply of care by helping to recruit and retain qualified providers. Some fifteen hundred companies nationwide offer their employees such services. They supplement the services with parenting seminars, support groups, handbooks, hot lines, and caregiver fairs.

Vouchers

In a voucher system, the company subsidizes a percentage of parents' child care costs at programs selected by the parents. The company may pay the provider directly or reimburse the employee. The value of the voucher may be offered as a flat fee or a percentage of cost, or it can be limited to those below a certain income level.

Discounts

Some companies negotiate employee discounts with child care providers. Typically a child care center lowers its fee by 10 percent and the employer contributes 10 percent of the fees, so the employees receive a 20 percent reduction in their child care costs.

Programs for Part-Time or Emergency Care

Because school and work hours vary, attention to the needs of school-aged children after school can reduce parental worry on the job. Employers can support after-school programs in the public schools or in community agencies. Employers can also sponsor "warm lines"—call-in services that provide assistance or reassurance to older children at home alone—or seminars that help children learn skills for staying at home alone. Companies may also provide reimbursement for child care costs incurred by work-related travel.

Care for Sick Children

Employers may opt to participate in a number of ways with a sick-child care policy. They may make arrangements with a health-care facility to provide in-home care for mildly ill children and subsidize part of the cost based on family income. They may also provide contributions or make arrangements with hospital sick-care facilities or community agencies for the care of mildly ill children. Employers may opt to provide funds to help local child care centers create their own sick-bay facilities. Finally, employers may provide sanctioned personal or family leave days so employees may remain at home with sick dependents.

Dependent Care Spending Assistance Plan (DCAP)

This plan deducts money from the employee's gross salary and places it into a nontaxable spending account. The employee then pays for any child care expenses with the tax-free dollars. Neither the employer nor employee pays taxes on this deducted amount.

Odd-Hour Care

Because of varying work schedules, an employer may provide in-home or center-based care for children during nontraditional work hours, such as weekend or night shifts.

Government/State Takeover

This thought provokes immediate delight or fear, depending on whom you are talking to. Where does influence stop benefiting and start imposing? This is a topic that you will continue to hear more about in years to come. Availability is exciting, but mandatory attendance is too often the next step:

- Mandatory kindergarten programs are becoming widespread.
- Mandatory full-day kindergarten is around the corner.
- Preschool programs and state-funded prekindergarten (Pre-K) programs for three- to five-year-olds are popping up in communities nationwide.
- Mandatory Pre-K programs are being discussed.
- Infant and toddler programs are flourishing.
- What about mandatory programs for children starting from birth?

There is a joy in watching good early childhood programs made available to all children and their parents from birth through elementary school age. There is more job security, advancement, and professionalism obtained by child care providers, teachers, and educators by supported child care programs. But where does the availability of programs stop and mandatory attendance start? The responsibility seems a little unclear.

Probably the biggest push for government-supported full-day programs for children under six years of age is that more families have parents working full-time. They need a safe, clean, and quality place for their children. Team that thought with the government's desire that all children who enter school are ready to learn. With that, you almost have a guarantee of continued growth of and support for early childhood programs.

Child care careers are under an umbrella of great change and upward mobility. Without government or community support, child care programs won't make it. If you enter child care—in whatever chosen field—you will have a part in affecting which direction and how far government intervention goes.

Unions and Labor Laws

What issues do unions address? According to the article "Union Presidents Speak Out on Child Care," printed in Working for America Institute's 2003 publication *Connections*, the child care issues that unions are addressing are as follows:

Lack of training opportunities
Low salaries and minmal benefits
High turnover
Low state-reimbursement rates

In the past few years, efforts to organize child care workers and family child care providers have increased. The following three unions have had success in the child care industry:

American Federation of State, County, and
  Municipal Employees (AFSCME)
1625 L Street NW
Washington, DC 20036-5687
www.afscme.org

California Federation of Teachers (CFT)
One Kaiser Plaza, Suite 1440
Oakland, CA 94612
www.cft.org

Service Employees International Union (SEIU)
1313 L Street NW
Washington, DC 20005
www.seiu.org

Visit their websites for more information and updates on their growing efforts in these areas. Other than unions, there are state labor laws that regulate what the minimum wages are and federal laws that govern discrimination policies. Your state employment offices (workforce centers) should be able to provide information on these regulations.

You can contact the Center for the Child Care Workforce as well as the National Labor Relations Board for lists of their publications (available online). Information on how to contact your state labor board is also available on the National Labor Relations Board's website.

Center for the Child Care Workforce
555 New Jersey Avenue NW
Washington, DC 20001
www.ccw.org

National Labor Relations Board
1099 Fourteenth Street NW
Washington, DC 20570-0001
www.nlrb.gov

Job Outlook

The U.S. Department of Labor's publications *Employer and Child Care: Establishing Services through the Workplace* and *Women in the Labor Force: A Data Book* state that the child-care needs for children of working parents have been increasing greatly since World War II. This increase is because more mothers of minor children are entering the labor force. The following percentages are of all women (with children under the age of eighteen) who were employed in the year indicated.

1940	8.6 percent
1982	58.5 percent
1984	60.5 percent
1988	65.1 percent
1990	66.7 percent
1995	69.7 percent
2000	72.9 percent
2004	70.1 percent

In 2004, 59.5 percent of children under the age of six had both parents in the labor force. Through 2012 the number of women of childbearing age (widely considered to be ages fifteen to forty-four) is expected to grow slowly; however, their participation in the work force is expected to increase. Women with young children are almost as likely as other women to work. Also, women are returning to work sooner after childbirth. In addition to this, the number of children under the age of five is expected to increase between 2002 and 2012. Because of these and other facts, the employment of child day-care service workers is projected to increase 43 percent over the 2002–12 period.

Child care has become a basic part of American families as more and more women have entered the labor force as sole supporters of their families or because of the need for two incomes in the family. In 1987, 40 percent of American three- and four-year-olds were in some kind of preschool group. This was three times the number in 1965. Also, one-third of all preschoolers in these groups (nursery school, Head Start, or child care centers) had mothers at home. In 2001 more than twelve million children under the age of six spent part of their day being cared for by someone other than a parent. (See Figure 6.1.)

Child care workers are going to be needed in many different fields. Over the past three decades, the number of women in the labor force has grown tremendously, especially the number of married women with young children. In 2004, 62.2 percent of all women with preschool-aged children were in the labor force, compared with 12 percent in 1950.

The Child Life Council also discussed information about job opportunities in the *Opportunities Child Life: Career and Program Information* pamphlet. Child-life careers are for those interested in working in a health-care setting. Job opportunities in child-life careers exist throughout the United States and Canada, but they are still limited because of cost. Health-care facilities need further education concerning the effectiveness of child-life programs in meeting the emotional and developmental needs of children and families. Salaries are similar to those of entry-level school teachers but vary greatly depending upon the institution and the setting. It

Figure 6.1 Percentage of Children Ages 0–6 Not Yet in Kindergarten, by Type of Care Arrangement, 2001

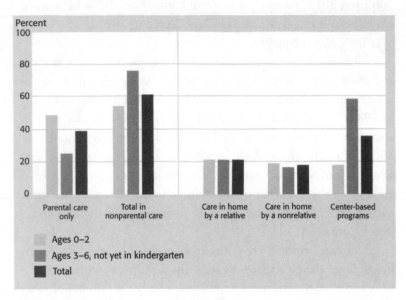

Source: Federal Interagency Forum on Child and Family Statistics. *America's Children: Key National Indicators of Well-Being*, 2005. Federal Interagency Forum on Child and Family Statistics, Washington, DC: U.S. Government Printing Office. On the Internet at http://child stats.ed.gov/pubs.asp.

is stated that although the positions are limited at this point, the educational preparation of the specialists is applicable to a wide variety of work with children and families.

Need for Supporting Child Care

According to the U.S. Census Bureau's 2004 American Community Survey, 8.3 million families with children under the age of eighteen were maintained by women. Of these families, 37.6 percent had an income below the poverty level. Single-parent families (families with only one parent residing in the household) are continuing to become a larger segment of all families. This is especially true for those families maintained by women.

Child Care Earnings

In 2002 there were 1.2 million child care workers in the United States; 14 percent were employed as private household workers, and 16 percent were working in family or center-based child care services. The remaining 70 percent mostly worked in local government educational services, nursing and residential care facilities, religious organizations, recreation industries, private educational services, civic and social organizations, and individual and family services. The median hourly earnings of child care workers in 2002 were $7.86. The middle 50 percent earned between $6.66 and $9.65 an hour. The highest 10 percent earned more than $11.46 an hour and the lowest 10 percent earned less than $5.91 an hour.

The average weekly earnings of full-time child day-care service providers in 2002 were $284. Full-time prekindergarten and kindergarten teachers earned an average of $8.69 an hour. Earnings of self-employed child care workers vary depending on the hours worked, numbers and ages of children, and the geographic area.

7

Organizations and Other Support Services

Turnover in child care fields is high. Stress is high. One thing that can help focus a person's concerns and energies in a positive direction is the help of supportive groups and services. Services can help improve working conditions and perhaps even salaries. Groups can help re-create the original drive and enthusiasm in the child care worker that isolation and unprofessional attitudes may have exhausted.

Local Organizations

One of the best support groups is a local organization that can meet regularly to discuss immediate, local, and ongoing concerns. It may have a membership fee and may provide other services. Usually there are two kinds of local support groups: One is where providers meet to discuss problems and make services available to members; it is a problem-solving, emotionally supportive, learning group.

The other type of group may provide training and services to meet the needs of its members but sees itself as a service organization. It may give parties for disadvantaged children, help with fundraisers for needy causes, or provide volunteer services. Examples of such services may be providing gifts for children in hospitals at Christmas or raising money for the March of Dimes.

A group might start off being an emotional support group and grow into a service-oriented group. The direction a group goes depends upon the leadership and the vocal members of the group. An ideal group would be one that meets for emotional support and forms committees to support other interests. Unfortunately, a group often becomes one kind or the other.

Contact local licensing agencies for addresses and names of related child care support groups. Colleges, other schools, or professional organizations might also have more information about local child care support groups relating to your specific area of interest. Online support groups can also be very helpful. With the Internet, it is easy for child care workers to connect to discuss frustrations, share ideas, and support one another without leaving their homes. The participants of these groups could be from around the world or within a centralized area. Look for local chat rooms, online bulletin boards, and ListServs.

State Child Care Organizations

Many states have an organization that runs independently or cooperatively with local groups. The advantage of a state organization is that it usually has more information and resources available. Its voice advocating for all child care providers, nursery school teachers, special needs, or educators speaks louder than local or county groups for affecting legislation and in changing regulations. A child care organization may also offer the following services:

Store discounts
Group insurance
Up-to-date legislative information
Field trips
Food programs
Substitute providers
Emotional support
Fellowship

Contact local licensing agencies for state child care associations. Also contact child-development, specialty training, or educational departments for related state organizations. See the list of child care organizations, associations, and agencies listed in Chapter 8. Journals and newsletters are also good sources of information about state and national associations.

Newsletters and Publications

Next to support groups, learning and sharing ideas and concerns through local and national newsletters or other publications is a great way of keeping informed. Topic may include the following:

Activities for children
Curriculum ideas
Arts and crafts
Information from other professionals
Local, state, and national child care concerns

Legislation affecting child care
Problem-solving ideas
Nutritional information
Time-saving hints

See Chapter 8 for references and the Bibliography for publications. Check with community action and Head Start preschool programs, and community/vocational/technical colleges, universities, and training programs for available newsletters.

Lending Libraries (Toys and Resources)

Supplies such as toys, children's books, resource books, car seats, crafts supplies, safety devices, and periodicals might be available for loan or at low cost for an annual fee in a local organization. This could help decrease initial costs for supplies.

Contact local licensing agencies for toy and resource lending libraries that might be available locally. Also check with other child care programs and child care associations for references.

Training

Classes and workshops might be available through local licensing agencies, community education classes, local nonprofit child care organizations, and local support groups for free, a membership fee, or a nominal cost. This could help supplement and provide training for child care workers and supportive staff in a number of areas:

First aid and CPR   Fire safety
Child development   Home safety

Arts and crafts	Gaining professional status
Income tax	Record keeping
Nutrition	Behavior management
Curriculum ideas	Parent relationships

Public Library

Another great resource available to most communities is the public library. You may borrow materials and books or participate in programs and services set up at the library. Most of these services are free or at very low cost and include:

Books	Storytelling
CDs/cassettes	Puppet shows
CD-ROMs	Book fairs
DVDs/videocassettes	Reading programs
Pictures	Films/projectors
Meeting rooms	Full reference section
Arts and crafts books	Business-related books

Services may vary somewhat with the size of your library and whether it is a main library, a branch, or a bookmobile. Check in the phone book or online for the nearest public library. Also, check for permission to use private, law, or college libraries.

The Child and Adult Care Food Program

The Child and Adult Care Food Program (CACFP) is part of the National School Lunch Act, offering cash reimbursement and donated commodities to child care facilities that serve food. The program promotes well-balanced meals for preschoolers in the child-care facilities. They receive reimbursement for up to two meals and one snack per child each day.

The kinds of foods and menus vary, although they have to meet U.S. Department of Agriculture (USDA) guidelines for nutrition. Nationally, the program is administered by the Department of Education or other state agencies. In nine states, the USDA administers the program through its Food and Nutrition Service Regional Offices.

In 1975 CACFP was amended to include licensed or approved family child care homes. Where licensing or approval is not available, providers meeting USDA standards may participate. In 2004, $2.02 billion were reimbursed to institutions participating in CACFP. In September 2004 alone, CACFP provided meals to three million children and eighty-six thousand adults.

Each month the provider completes appropriate forms and is reimbursed by the sponsor. Payment depends upon the number of meals and snacks that are served during the month multiplied by the reimbursement rate. The provider has certain responsibilities, including: to serve meals that meet USDA requirements, to submit monthly attendance and menu forms, to sign written agreements with the sponsor organization, and to reapply annually for program participation.

To find out more about these programs and eligibility guidelines, contact appropriate licensing agencies or the U.S. Department of Agriculture:

U.S. Department of Agriculture
Food and Nutrition Service
3101 Park Center Drive
Alexandria, VA 22302
www.fns.usda.gov

Funding Sources

The Women's Bureau has prepared a book entitled *Employers and Child Care: Establishing Services Through the Workplace*. This book describes many supportive and funding sources. The following summarizes some of these sources.

Child Care Funding

Some funding is available through government funding for children of families at or near poverty levels. This funding is available to for-profit centers, not-for-profit centers, and family child care homes to provide child care services for these children. Contact your county welfare or social services departments for information and guidelines if you will be serving low-income parents.

Other Funding

State job-training programs may provide money for training child care workers:

> Department of Education
> 400 Maryland Avenue SW
> Washington, DC 20202
> www.ed.gov
> (work-study programs through colleges)

> U.S. Department of Labor
> Employment and Training Administration
> 200 Constitution Avenue NW
> Washington, DC 20210
> www.doleta.gov
> (Job Training and Partnership Act, job training, and summer youth
>   programs)

Another way to gain services for child care programs is through agreements with nearby high schools, colleges, or specialized institutions. If your program has a good curriculum with experienced staff, students may be placed at centers for volunteer or work-study experiences. If you are a student or going to be, this also may be a way to get practical experience. Nursing students may make vision or hearing checks, while developmental child care or teaching students might offer additional services. Also check with high school career counselors, vocational schools' placement or work experience offices, and college placement or career offices.

Many child care organizations and agencies have been mentioned throughout this book. Contact the ones that most closely represent the area that you are thinking of entering. There is a wealth of support and information out there, as well as many people and professionals eager to share their knowledge and experience with you.

8

ADDITIONAL RESOURCES

You CAN LEARN a lot about specific areas of child care by becoming familiar with related associations, organizations, and agencies. Read their journals, newsletters, and other printed materials to help you better understand their philosophies and concerns. Send a self-addressed stamped envelope with a request for information to the association or office in your area of interest, or visit their websites.

U.S. Associations and Organizations

Here are some associations and organizations to get you started.

Adults & Childrens Alliance
2885 Country Drive, Suite 165
St. Paul, MN 55117-2621
www.acainc.org

This nonprofit corporation offers resources and services designed to meet the changing needs of child care professionals, parents, and the community. It is one of the largest child care provider groups in the United States. It offers liability insurance, newsletters, business information, an equipment exchange service, classes and workshops, and individual consultation for members.

American Montessori Society, Inc. (AMS)
281 Park Avenue South
New York, NY 10010-6102
www.amshq.org

This educational membership organization supports the Montessori method of learning. It offers information on Montessori and requirements and programs for obtaining a Montessori credential.

Association for Childhood Education International (ACEI)
17904 Georgia Avenue, Suite 215
Olney, MD 20832
www.acei.org

ACEI is an international association that is concerned with child care and interested in promoting good educational practices for children, infancy through early adolescence.

Association Montessori International/USA (AMI)
410 Alexander Street
Rochester, NY 14607-1028
http://ami.edu/usa

This is an international Montessori association.

Center for the Child Care Workforce (CCW)
555 New Jersey Avenue NW
Washington, DC 20001
www.ccw.org

The CCW (formally called the Child Care Employee Project) is a nonprofit organization that provides resources and assistance to child care workers to upgrade their status and working conditions. Topics and materials include substitute and break policies, grievances, procedures, occupational health and safety, employment rights, staff relations, working with directors, unionizing, staff evaluations, and more.

Child Care Law Center
22 Second Street
San Francisco, CA 94105
www.childcarelaw.org
The Child Care Law Center serves as a legal resource for the local, state, and national child care communities. Its purpose is to foster the development of quality, affordable child care programs.

Child Life Council, Inc. (CLC)
11820 Parklawn Drive, Suite 240
Rockville, MD 20852
www.childlife.org
CLC is composed of child-life specialists and others who use play, recreation, education, self-expression, and theories of child development to promote psychological well-being and optimum development in children, adolescents, and their families in health-care settings.

Child Welfare League of America, Inc.
440 First Street NW, Third Floor
Washington, DC 20001-2085
www.cwla.org

This is a national membership-based organization promoting the well-being of children and their families. Its primary objective is to make children a national priority. Of special concern are the unmet needs of children lacking physical, emotional, and intellectual care and nurturing. It provides information on all aspects of child welfare services.

Children's Defense Fund
25 East Street NW
Washington, DC 20001
www.childrensdefense.org

The Children's Defense Fund is a resource organization that influences legislation and regulatory and administrative policies on child care and other child-related issues.

Clearinghouse on Early Education and Parenting (CEEP)
Children's Research Center
51 Gerty Drive
Champaign, IL 61820-7469
http://ceep.crc.uiuc.edu

CEEP is the successor to the ERIC Clearinghouse on Elementary and Early Childhood Education. This organization provides online access to the ERIC/EECE archived materials through its website. Specific information about young children, development, and education is also available online.

Council for Professional Recognition
2460 Sixteenth Street NW
Washington, DC 20009-3575
www.cdacouncil.org

The council promotes quality child care through the Child Development Associate (CDA) credential program. Request information about the credential awarded to child care providers who demonstrate CDA competencies in their work with children, parents, and staff.

Early Childhood and Parenting Collaborative (ECAP)
University of Illinois
Children's Research Center
51 Gerty Drive
Champaign, IL 61820-7469
http://ecap.crc.uiuc.edu

The ECAP is home to more than a dozen research, technical assistance, and service projects that focus on the education, care, and parenting of young children, including the Clearinghouse on Early Education and Parenting (listed above).

International Child Resource Institute
1581 Leroy Avenue
Berkeley, CA 94708
www.icrichild.org

This is a nonprofit organization that promotes exchange of information on critical needs and issues facing children nationwide. It provides research assistance and written material.

International Nanny Association
2020 Southwest Freeway, Suite 208
Houston, TX 77098
www.nanny.org

This educational association is for nannies, nanny employers, nanny educators, nanny placement agencies, and providers of special services related to the nanny profession. It promotes in-home professional child care and serves as a clearinghouse of information on nannies.

National Association of Child Care Resources and Referral Agencies
3101 Wilson Boulevard, Suite 350
Arlington, VA 22201
www.naccrra.org
This organization is for community-based child care resources and referral agencies that promote a diverse, high-quality child care system with parental choice that is accessible to all families.

National Association for the Education of Young Children
    (NAEYC)
Resources for Early Childhood Professionals
1509 Sixteenth Street NW
Washington, DC 20036
www.naeyc.org
A membership organization dedicated to promoting excellence in early childhood education. It is the largest early childhood professional association that provides educational services and resources to child care workers. It offers conferences, accreditation, posters, videos, books, pamphlets, and other child care information.

National Association for Family Child Care
5202 Pinemont Drive
Salt Lake City, UT 84123
www.nafcc.org
This association is for family and group child care home providers and advocates across the country. It offers accreditation for family and group child care providers.

National Black Child Development Institute
1101 Fifteenth Street NW, Suite 900
Washington, DC 20005
www.nbcdi.org

This is a membership organization that acts as an advocate for black children and their families.

National Coalition for Campus Children's Centers
119 Schindler Education Center
University of Northern Iowa
Cedar Falls, IA 50614
www.campuschildren.org

This is a membership organization that promotes and provides support for both the concept and the reality of high-quality child care on campuses. It offers a conference, a list of child-care providers on campuses, consultation, support group, and information on how to start a campus child care center.

Parent Cooperative Preschools International (PCPI)
National Cooperative Business Center
1401 New York Avenue NW, Suite 1100
Washington, DC 20005
http://preschools.coop

This is a service organization for member co-op preschools, teachers, and parents. It provides a member directory, support through an established network, a resource catalog, and referral information. It also offers an online discussion group, website links for schools/groups and councils, brochures and pamphlets, and a regular informational journal.

Redleaf National Institute
10 Yorkton Court
St. Paul, MN 55117
www.redleafinstitute.org

This nonprofit organization helps child care providers successfully manage their businesses. It offers support to trainers of providers, tax preparers, and organizations that assist providers with their business. In addition it makes available training opportunities and publishes books, articles, pamphlets, and other materials to assist family child care providers in their development.

Canadian Associations and Organizations

The following are brief summaries of some of the associations and organizations and their addresses that people interested in child care services in Canada may contact for more information. Canadians face similar problems and concerns in the area of child care and education. Their provinces (like U.S. states) also face the problems of unifying standards. Contact an organization in the area where you live and of the type of child care in which you are interested. Child Care Online has a valuable website for information on child care in Canada. Visit www.childcare.net.

Alberta Association of Services for Children and Families
Box 130, Suite 945, Phipps Mckinnon Building
10020-101A Avenue
Edmonton, AB T5J 3G2
www.aascf.com
This association's goal is to organize and represent child welfare and family service providers by developing standards dedicated to residential and community child care services, influencing social policy and legislation, and creating a network of support agencies.

Alvin Buckwold Early Childhood Intervention Program
Kinsmen Children's Centre
1319 Colony Street
Saskatoon, SK S7J 2ZI
www.saskatoonhealthregion.ca/your_health/facilities_kinsmen_early
   _childhood.htm

This program strives to promote and foster the general welfare and individual rights of children from birth to five years of age who are at risk for developmental delay and of children with disabilities. Its mission is to promote the development of high-quality early childhood intervention services for these children and their families, to represent the interests of early childhood intervention services to the government of Saskatchewan and other related service providers, and to conduct and/or facilitate programs on evaluation and research.

Association for Early Childhood Educators, Ontario
40 Orchard View Boulevard, #211
Toronto, ON M4R 1B9
www.cfc-efc.ca/aeceo
This association supports the needs and goals of the early childhood educators in Ontario by offering opportunities for professional and personal growth.

Canada Council on Child and Youth Care Associations
2211 Riverside Drive, Suite 11
Ottawa, ON K1H 7X5
www.cyccanada.ca
This council serves as a coordinating and networking organization for provincial and territorial child and youth care associations. It promotes development of child and youth care as a profession in Canada and encourages the delivery of quality care.

The Canadian Association for Young Children
#302-1775 West 11th Avenue
Vancouver, BC V6J 2C1
www.cayc.ca

This association promotes and provides professional development opportunities for child care providers and has a support network for all child development programs.

Canadian Child Care Federation
201–83 Parkdale Avenue
Ottawa, ON K1Y 4R4
www.cccf-fcsge.ca

This group works to improve the quality of child care services for Canadian families by: implementing services to the child care community, supporting the development of provincial/territorial organizations, and enhancing skills of individuals working in the child care field. It is a bilingual, nonprofit organization committed to excellence in early learning and child care.

Child Care Advocacy Association of Canada
714-151 Slater Street
Ottawa, ON K1P 5H3
www.childcareadvocacy.ca

The goal of this association is to build a consensus across Canada to achieve a comprehensive system of accessible, affordable, and high-quality nonprofit child care.

Child and Youth Care Association of Alberta
12013-76 Street, #204
Edmonton, AB T5B 2C9
www.cycaa.com

This association works to promote, improve, and maintain progressive standards of child/youth care services and to encourage an active public interest in child/youth care services.

Council of Parent Participation
Preschools in British Columbia
4340 Carson Street, #4
Burnaby, BC V5J 2X9
www.cpppreschools.bc.ca

The council helps to promote a high standard of education for preschoolers (three and four years of age) and also a planned adult education program through the cooperative efforts of parents and supervisors.

Manitoba Child Care Association (MCCA)
2350 McPhillips Street, 2nd Floor
Winnipeg, MB R2V 4J5
www.mccahouse.org

The aim of this association is to advocate for a quality system of child care, advance early childhood education as a profession, and provide member services.

Ontario Coalition for Better Child Care
726 Bloor Street West, Suite 209
Toronto, ON M6G 4A1
www.childcareontario.org

This umbrella group comprises provincial organizations and provincial sections of national organizations of local child care advocacy groups, parents, child care programs, union locals, and women's groups. It promotes the use of a variety of child care supports that enable families to fulfill their obligations. It lobbies for improvement in the child care system, prepares briefs for the government, coordinates the activities of local coalitions, and organizes conferences, workshops, and demonstrations.

Parent Cooperative Preschools International
3767 Northwood Drive
Niagara Falls, ON L2H 2Y5
http://preschools.coop

This cooperative works to promote the awareness of preschool education, to provide education for parents of preschoolers, to provide desired standards of programs, and to study and promote legislation designed to further the health of children and families.

Agencies

Government agencies are also a good resource for information.

Department of Education
400 Maryland Avenue SW
Washington, DC 20202-0310
www.ed.gov

Information is available on work-study opportunities through colleges. This department may also refer you to appropriate state agencies. Information may also be available on block grants, laws, and regulations concerning early childhood education.

Department of Health and Human Services
National Child Care Information Center
10530 Rosehaven Street, Suite 400
Fairfax, VA 22030
http://nccic.acf.hhs.gov

This department may offer some information on child care services. However, because the responsibility of child care is with the states, contact your state child care licensing administrators for your state's specific regulations and services. Also, ask for your local licensing agency. This will usually be your county welfare department or county social services. This agency works toward improvement of child care services in three major areas: Head Start, Children's Bureau, and youth development.

Education Commission of the States
Early Learning Project
700 Broadway, #1200
Denver, CO 80203-3460
www.ecs.org

The commission provides information on early learning issues and state policies.

National Clearinghouse on Child Abuse and Neglect Information
Children's Bureau
Administration on Children, Youth, and Families
370 L'Enfant Promenade SW
Washington, DC 20447
http://nccanch.acf.hhs.gov

This government-sponsored clearinghouse collects, organizes, and makes available information on all aspects of child abuse and neglect.

National Labor Relations Board (NLRB)
1099 Fourteenth Street NW
Washington, DC 20570-0001
www.nlrb.gov

This independent federal agency provides information on labor laws and other references.

U.S. Department of Agriculture
Food and Nutrition Service (FNS)
Child Nutrition
Special Nutrition Programs
3101 Park Center Drive
Alexandria, VA 22302
www.fns.usda.gov/cnd

Contact this agency regarding the Child Care Food Program, nutrition education and training, in-service training of food service, and teaching personnel. The FNS works to empower program participants with knowledge of the link between diet and health.

U.S. Department of Labor
Employment and Training Administration
200 Constitution Avenue NW
Washington, DC 20210
www.doleta.gov

Contact this department for information on the job training partnership act, job training, and summer youth training.

U.S. Small Business Administration
409 Third Street SW
Washington, DC 20416
www.sba.gov

Contact the SBA to find local contacts and information on starting a business.

Women's Bureau
Department of Labor
Frances Perkins Building
200 Constitution Avenue NW
Washington, DC 20210
www.dol.gov/wb
This agency helps promote women in the workforce with statistics, brochures, pamphlets, publication lists, and technical assistance.

Periodicals, Journals, and Newsletters

Publications of organizations are valuable reference materials. You will learn more about what is happening in the field of child care and about specific areas of interest by reading them. Listed below are some magazines, journals, and newsletters and the association that publishes them.

The Black Child Advocate (quarterly newsletter), NBCDI
CDF Reports (legislative updates), Children's Defense Fund
Child Care Bulletin (quarterly online newsletter), NCCIC
Child Development (journal), Society for Research in Child
    Development
Child Welfare (bimonthly journal), CWLA
Childhood Education (journal), ACEI
Communication (journal), AMI
Connections (newsletter), National Network for Child Care
Cooperative Speaking (newsletter), PCPI
Exchange (magazine), Child Care Information Exchange
Legal Update (quarterly newsletter), Child Care Law
    Center

Montessori Life (quarterly magazine), AMS

YC Young Children (journal), NAEYC

Related Associations and Councils

Child care careers are related to and sometimes overlap other helping careers. The following are references to help you explore some of these related areas:

Psychiatry

American Psychiatric Association
1000 Wilson Boulevard, Suite 1825
Arlington, VA 22209-3901
www.psych.org

Council on Medical Education
American Medical Association
515 North State Street
Chicago, IL 60610
www.ama-assn.org

Psychology

American Psychological Association
750 First Street NE
Washington, DC 20002-4242
www.apa.org

National Health Council
1730 M Street NW, Suite 500
Washington, DC 20036
www.nationalhealthcouncil.org

Social Work

Council on Social Work Education
1725 Duke Street, Suite 300
Alexandria, VA 22314-3457
www.cswe.org

National Association of Social Workers
750 First Street NE, Suite 700
Washington, DC 20002-4241
www.naswdc.org

Nursing

American Nurse Association
8515 Georgia Avenue, Suite 400
Silver Spring, MD 20910
www.nursingworld.org

National League for Nursing
61 Broadway
New York, NY 10006
www.nln.org

Recreation Work/Therapy

National Recreation and Park Association
22377 Belmont Ridge Road
Ashburn, VA 20148
www.nrpa.org

Music Therapy

American Music Therapy Association, Inc.
8455 Colesville Road, Suite 1000
Silver Spring, MD 20910
www.musictherapy.org

Art Therapy

American Art Therapy Association
1202 Allanson Road
Mundelein, IL 60060-3808
www.arttherapy.org

Department of Defense—Child Development Programs

The following are points of contact for those interested in military child care programs:

All United States Military Branches
Military Family Resource Center
Crystal Square 4, Suite 302, Room 309
241 Eighteenth Street
Arlington, VA 22202-3424
www.mfrc-dodqol.org/mcy

Defense Logistics Agency
Morale Welfare and Recreation Office
Child and Youth Services
8725 John J. Kingman Road, Room 2545
Fort Belvoir, VA 22060-6221
www.dla.mil/dss/dss-q

United States Air Force
Headquarters, Air Force Services Agency
Chief, Child Development Branch
10100 Reunion Place, Suite 402
San Antonio, TX 78216-4138
www-p.afsv.af.mil/fmp

United States Army
U.S. Army Community and Family Support Center
ATTN: CFSC-CYS
4700 King Street, 4th Floor
Alexandria, VA 22302-4418
www.armymwr.com/portal/family/childandyouth

United States Coast Guard
Headquarters Support Command
CG Headquarters Child Development Center
2100 Second Street, SW
Washington, DC 20593-0001
www.uscg.mil/hq/g-w/g-wk/wkw/child_care/child
    _development_centers.htm

United States Marine Corps
Headquarters, United States Marine Corps
Personal and Family Readiness Division
3280 Russell Road
Quantico, VA 22134
www.usmc-mccs.org/cyt

United States National Guard
National Guard Family Program
1411 Jefferson Davis Highway
Arlington, VA 22202-3231
www.guardfamily.org

United States Navy
Navy Child and Youth Programs
Commander Navy Installations
5720 Integrity Drive
Millington, TN 38055
www.mwr.navy.mil/mwrprgms/commain.htm

For More Information

Many associations, organizations, and agencies have informational pamphlets that you can send for and receive free or at a low cost. Request a list of available publications from associations in your field of interest. See addresses listed earlier in this chapter. Enclose a self-addressed stamped envelope with your request, or request information through the association's website or by e-mail.

Other material may be bought through these and other organizations. They have valuable information in the form of books, pamphlets, audio and videotapes, CD-ROMs and DVDs. Their catalogs, brochures, or websites will describe what is available and give cost and ordering information. Specific information in various fields may be obtained this way. Here is an example of some of the materials available from associations.

National Association for the Education of Young Children (NAEYC)

The NAEYC's website at www.naeyc.org/pubs has information on books, brochures, posters, accreditation information, videos, and membership details. Specific titles like the following deal with the education of young children: *Developing Your Portfolio—Enhancing Your Learning and Showing Your Stuff: A Guide for the Early Childhood Student or Professional*; *Working in the Reggio Way: A Beginner's Guide for American Teachers*; and *Educating and Caring for Very Young Children: The Infant/Toddler Curriculum*.

Association for Childhood Education International

Visit the association's website at www.acei.org/resources.htm for information on education resources. Included is information on its journals: *Childhood Education* and *Journal of Research in Childhood Education*. Also available are books, brochures, position papers (ACEI's official view on current and important issues), reprints from *Childhood Education*, videotapes and audiotapes, and special items. On the association's website, you can also find information on memberships, conferences, and awards and grants.

Child Welfare League of America

CWLA's website (www.cwla.org/pubs) lists materials concerning child welfare services. The "CWLA Standards" (goals for the ongoing improvement of services for children) are available to order. Also listed are materials under the topics of administration and advocacy, adoption, family foster care, children's books, resident group care, child day care, child abuse and neglect, training resources, cultural competence, and more.

Child Care Law Center

Visit the Child Care Law Center online at www.childcarelaw.org/ publications.cfm. Listed is information such as "Child Care Contracts: Information for Providers;" "Legal Issues for Family Child Care Providers: Contracts;" "Caring for Children with HIV or AIDS in Child Care;" "A Child Care Advocacy Guide to Land Use Principles;" and "Caring for Children with Special Needs: The Americans with Disabilities Act (ADA) and Child Care."

9

EDUCATIONAL CONTACTS

YOU MAY WANT to contact an organization that serves your special interests for a list of recommended schools. (See Chapter 8 for addresses of organizations.) For example, for information regarding child-life specialists or work in child care within a health-care setting, contact the Child Life Council, Inc., or visit its website. This organization has a list of colleges that offer degrees/curriculums in child life. As of this date, the Child Life Council does not certify educational programs. Ask for its "Academic Programs/ Degrees/Curriculum in Child Life."

The American Montessori Society, Inc., or the Association Montessori International/USA will provide you with a list of approved schools or tell you whom to contact to learn the Montessori method of child care education.

The Council for Professional Recognition should be able to provide you with cooperating schools and institutions with Child Development Associate credentialing programs.

Community/Vocational/Technical Institutions

To find out about courses at your local community/vocational/technical institutions, contact your state office of higher education. Libraries, school counselors, and career guidance personnel may have this information, too.

State Offices of Higher Education

Alabama
Commission on Higher Education
P.O. Box 302000
Montgomery, AL 36130-2000
www.ache.state.al.us

Alaska
Commission on Postsecondary Education
AlaskAdvantage Programs
3030 Vintage Boulevard
Juneau, AK 99801-7100
http://alaskaadvantage.state.ak.us

Arizona
Commission for Postsecondary Education
2020 North Central Avenue, Suite 550
Phoenix, AZ 85004-4503
www.azhighered.org

Arkansas
Department of Higher Education
114 East Capitol
Little Rock, AR 72201-3818
www.arkansashighered.com

California

California Student Aid Commission
P.O. Box 419027
Rancho Cordova, CA 95741-9027
www.csac.ca.gov

Colorado

Commission on Higher Education
1380 Lawrence Street, Suite 1200
Denver, CO 80203
www.state.co.us/cche

Connecticut

Department of Higher Education
61 Woodland Street
Hartford, CT 06105-2326
www.ctdhe.org

Delaware

Higher Education Commission
Carvel State Office Building, 5th Floor
820 North French Street
Wilmington, DE 19801
www.doe.state.de.us/high-ed

District of Columbia

State Education Office
Government of the District of Columbia
One Judiciary Square
441 Fourth Street NW, Suite 350 North
Washington, DC 20001
http://seo.dc.gov/main.shtm

Florida

State University System of Florida
107 West Gaines Street, Suite 1614
Tallahassee, FL 32399
www.flbog.org

Georgia

Georgia Student Finance Commission
State Loans Division
2082 East Exchange Place, Suite 230
Tucker, GA 30084
www.gsfc.org

Hawaii

State Postsecondary Education Commission
2444 Dole Street, Room 209
Honolulu, HI 96822-2302
www.wiche.edu/states/hi.asp

Idaho

State Board of Education
P.O. Box 83720
Boise, ID 83720-0037
www.boardofed.idaho.gov

Illinois

State Student Assistance Commission of Illinois
1755 Lake Cook Road
Deerfield, IL 60015-5209
www.collegezone.com

Indiana

> State Student Assistance Commission of Indiana
> 150 West Market Street, Suite 500
> Indianapolis, IN 46204-2811
> www.ssaci.in.gov

Iowa

> Iowa College Student Aid Commission
> 200 Tenth Street, 4th Floor
> Des Moines, IA 50319-3609
> www.iowacollegeaid.org

Kansas

> Kansas Board of Regents
> Curtis State Office Building
> 1000 SW Jackson Street, Suite 520
> Topeka, KS 66612-1368
> www.kansasregents.org

Kentucky

> Kentucky Higher Education Assistance Authority
> P.O. Box 798
> Frankfort, KY 40602-0798
> www.kheaa.com

Louisiana

> Office of Student Financial Assistance
> P.O. Box 91202
> Baton Rouge, LA 70821-9202
> www.osfa.state.la.us

Maine

Finance Authority of Maine
5 Community Drive
P.O. Box 949
Augusta, ME 04332-0949
www.famemaine.com

Maryland

Maryland Higher Education Commission
839 Bestgate Road, Suite 400
Annapolis, MD 21401-1024
www.mhec.state.md.us

Massachusetts

Massachusetts Board of Higher Education
One Ashburton Place, Room 1401
Boston, MA 02108-1696
www.mass.edu

Michigan

Michigan Higher Education Assistance Authority
Office of Scholarships and Grants
P.O. Box 30462
Lansing, MI 48909-7962
www.michigan.gov/mistudentaid

Minnesota

Office of Higher Education
1450 Energy Park Drive, Suite 350
St. Paul, MN 55108-5227
www.ohe.state.mn.us

Mississippi

Office of Student Financial Aid
3825 Ridgewood Road
Jackson, MS 39211-6453
www.mississippiuniversities.com

Missouri

State Department of Higher Education
3515 Amazonas Drive
Jefferson City, MO 65109
www.dhe.mo.gov

Montana

Office of Higher Education
Montana University System
46 North Last Chance Gulch
P.O. Box 203201
Helena, MT 59620-3201
www.montana.edu/wwwoche

Nebraska

Coordinating Commission for Postsecondary Education
140 North Eighth Street, Suite 300
P.O. Box 95005
Lincoln, NE 68509-5005
www.ccpe.state.ne.us/publicdoc/ccpe

Nevada

Nevada System of Higher Education
5550 West Flamingo Road, Suite C-1
Las Vegas, NV 89103
www.nevada.edu

New Hampshire

State Postsecondary Education Commission
3 Barrell Court, Suite 300
Concord, NH 03301-8543
www.nh.gov/postsecondary

New Jersey

Commission on Higher Education
20 West State Street, Seventh Floor
P.O. Box 542
Trenton, NJ 08625-0542
www.state.nj.us/highereducation

Higher Education Student Assistance Authority
Building 4
Quakerbridge Plaza
P.O. Box 540
Trenton, NJ 08625-0540
www.hesaa.org

New Mexico

New Mexico Higher Education Department
1068 Cerrillos Road
Santa Fe, NM 87505
http://hed.state.nm.us

New York

New York State Higher Education Services Corporation
99 Washington Avenue
Albany, NY 12255
www.hesc.org

North Carolina

State Education Assistance Authority
P.O. Box 14103
Research Triangle Park, NC 27709-3663
www.cfnc.org

North Dakota

North Dakota University System
North Dakota Student Financial Assistance Program
10th Floor, State Capitol
600 East Boulevard Avenue, Department 215
Bismarck, ND 58505-0230
www.ndus.edu

Ohio

Ohio Board of Regents
State Grants and Scholarships Department
30 East Broad Street, 36th Floor
Columbus, OH 43215-3414
www.regents.state.oh.us/sgs

Oklahoma

Oklahoma State Regents for Higher Education
655 Research Parkway, Suite 200
Oklahoma City, OK 73104
www.okhighered.org

Oregon

Oregon Student Assistance Commission
1500 Valley River Drive, Suite 100
Eugene, OR 97401
www.osac.state.or.us

Oregon University System
506 SW Mill, Suite 530
P.O. Box 751
Portland, OR 97207-0751
www.ous.edu

Pennsylvania

Office of Postsecondary and Higher Education
Department of Education
333 Market Street
Harrisburg, PA 17126-0333
www.pdehighered.state.pa.us/higher/site

Rhode Island

Office of Higher Education
301 Promenade Street
Providence, RI 02908-5748
www.ribghe.org

Rhode Island Higher Education Assistance Authority
560 Jefferson Boulevard
Warwick, RI 02886
www.riheaa.org

South Carolina

Commission on Higher Education
1333 Main Street, Suite 200
Columbia, SC 29201
www.che.sc.gov

South Dakota

South Dakota Board of Regents
306 East Capitol Avenue, Suite 200
Pierre, SD 57501-2545
www.ris.sdbor.edu

Tennessee

Tennessee Higher Education Commission
Parkway Towers Building, Suite 1900
404 James Robertson Parkway
Nashville, TN 37243-0830
www.state.tn.us/thec

Texas

Texas Higher Education Coordinating Board
1200 East Anderson Lane
P.O. Box 12788
Austin, TX 78711
www.thecb.state.tx.us

Utah

Utah State Board of Regents
Gateway Center
60 South 400 West
Salt Lake City, UT 84101-1284
www.utahsbr.edu

Vermont

Vermont Student Assistance Corporation
Champlain Mill
P.O. Box 2000
Winooski, VT 05404-2601
www.vsac.org

Virginia

Council of Higher Education
James Monroe Building
101 North Fourteenth Street, 9th Floor
Richmond, VA 23219
www.schev.edu

Washington

Higher Education Coordinating Board
917 Lakeridge Way
P.O. Box 43430
Olympia, WA 98504-3430
www.hecb.wa.gov

West Virginia

Higher Education Policy Commission
1018 Kanawha Boulevard East, Suite 700
Charleston, WV 25301-2800
www.hepc.wvnet.edu

Wisconsin

Higher Educational Aids Board (HEAB)
131 West Wilson Street, Suite 902
P.O. Box 7885
Madison, WI 53703
http://heab.state.wi.us

Wyoming

Wyoming Community College Commission
2020 Carey Avenue, 8th Floor
Cheyenne, WY 82002
www.commission.wcc.edu

Territories

American Samoa

American Samoa Community College
American Samoa Board of Higher Education
P.O. Box 2609
Pago Pago, AS 96799-2609
www.ascc.as

Commonwealth of the Northern Mariana Islands

Northern Marianas College
Olympio T. Borja Memorial Library
As-Terlaje Campus
P.O. Box 501250
Saipan, MP 96950-1250
www.nmcnet.edu

Guam

Guam Community College
P.O. Box 23069
Guam Main Facility, GU 96921
www.guamcc.net

Puerto Rico

Council on Higher Education
P.O. Box 19000
San Juan, PR 00910-1900
www.ces.gobierno.pr

Republic of the Marshall Islands

College of Marshall Islands
P.O. Box 1258
Majuro, MH 96960
www.cmiedu.net

Virgin Islands
Virgin Islands Department of Education
Office of Federal Programs
No. 44-46 Kongens Gades
Charlotte Amalie
St. Thomas, VI 00802
www.usvi.org/education

Additional Resources

The following resources will help you gather information and evaluate programs in the child care field.

Books
The College Blue Books by MacMillan Publishing Company
Fiske Guide to Colleges by Sourcebooks, Inc.

Websites
http://educationusa.state.gov
www.petersons.com

Also check under the section of "home economics" for parent educators. See sections highlighting education, child development, child care/child care management, or family-child studies for other options. Look for what degrees, special emphasis, and variations or concentrations are offered.

Direct School Contact

Whether you are considering one or a number of schools, contact each school directly to request a catalog, or visit the school's website. Look over the programs to see if you can fit in your areas of special interest, for example:

Prekindergarten, special education
Prekindergarten, sign language
Child development, special needs
Child care and management for in-home business

Write for more detailed information about each school's programs in child care, child development, early childhood education, or specialized child care. Aides or assistants are usually nine-month to one-year programs. People with two-year degrees are usually referred to as associates. Teachers must have a four-year degree, and specialists have more than four-year degrees. Terminology will vary.

Teacher Certification

Your local schools, school counselors, or college placement office should have information on what school requirements you need to obtain a preschool, prekindergarten, nursery, or other teaching position. You may also contact your State Teacher Certification Office in the list that follows for regulations that will affect you.

Addresses for State Offices of Certification

Alabama
State Department of Education
Teacher Education and Certification Office
50 North Ripley Street
P.O. Box 302101
Montgomery, AL 36130
www.alsde.edu

Alaska

State Department of Education
Teacher Education and Certification
Goldbelt Building
801 West Tenth Street, Suite 200
Juneau, AK 99801-1894
www.educ.state.ak.us/teachercertification

Arizona

State Department of Education
Teacher Certification Unit-016
1535 West Jefferson Street
P.O. Box 25609
Phoenix, AZ 85002
www.ade.state.az.us/certification

Arkansas

State Department of Education
Teacher Education and Licensure
#4 State Capitol Mall, Rooms 106B/107B
Little Rock, AR 72201-1071
http://arkedu.state.ar.us/teachers/teachers_licensure.html

California

Commission on Teacher Credentialing
1900 Capitol Avenue
P.O. Box 944270
Sacramento, CA 94244-2700
www.ctc.ca.gov/educator-prep

Colorado

State Department of Education
Educator Licensing Unit
201 East Colfax Avenue, Room 105
Denver, CO 80203-1704
www.cde.state.co.us/index_license.htm

Connecticut

State Department of Education
Bureau of Certification and Professional Development
P.O. Box 150471, Room 243
Hartford, CT 06115-0471
www.state.ct.us/sde

Delaware

State Department of Education
Office of Certification
Townsend Building
P.O. Box 1402
Dover, DE 19903-1402
www.udel.edu/teachered/delcert.html

District of Columbia

Teacher Education and Certification Branch
Logan Administration Building
215 G Street NE, Room 101A
Washington, DC 20002
www.k12.dc.us/dcps/home.html

Florida

State Department of Education
Bureau of Teacher Certification
Turlington Building
325 West Gaines Street, Room 201
Tallahassee, FL 32399-0400
www.fldoe.org/edcert

Georgia

Professional Standards Commission
Certification Section
1452 Twin Towers East
Atlanta, GA 30334
www.doe.k12.ga.us/doe/sboe

Hawaii

State Department of Education
Office of Personnel Services
Certification and Development Unit
Room 301
P.O. Box 2360
Honolulu, HI 96804
http://doe.k12.hi.us/personnel/teachinginhawaii.htm

Idaho

State Department of Education
Teacher Education and Certification
650 West State Street
P.O. Box 83720
Boise, ID 83720-0027
www.sde.state.id.us/certification

Illinois

Illinois Board of Teacher Education and Certification
100 North First Street
Springfield, IL 62777-0001
www.isbe.state.il.us

Indiana

State Department of Education
Division of Professional Standards
101 West Ohio Street, Suite 300
Indianapolis, IN 46204-2133
www.doe.state.in.us/dps

Iowa

Iowa State Board of Educational Examiners
Grimes State Office Building, Third Floor
Des Moines, IA 50310-0147
www.state.ia.us/boee

Kansas

State Department of Education
Office of Teacher Education and Certification
120 Southeast Tenth Avenue
Topeka, KS 66612-1182
www.ksde.org/cert/cert.html

Kentucky

State Department of Education
Division of Certification
Education Professional Standards Board
100 Airport Road, 3rd Floor
Frankfort, KY 40601
www.kyepsb.net

Louisiana

State Department of Education
Bureau of Higher Education and Teacher Certification
626 North Fourth Street
P.O. Box 94064
Baton Rouge, LA 70804-9064
www.doe.state.la.us/lde

Maine

State Department of Education
Division of Certification and Placement
23 State House Station
Augusta, ME 04333-0023
www.state.me.us/education/cert/cert.htm

Maryland

State Department of Education
Division of Certification and Accreditation
200 West Baltimore Street
Baltimore, MD 21201-2595
www.marylandpublicschools.org/MSDE/divisions/certification

Massachusetts

State Department of Education
Certification and Professional Development Coordination
350 Main Street
P.O. Box 9140
Malden, MA 02148-5023
www.doe.mass.edu/educators

Michigan

State Department of Education
Office of Professional Preparation and Certification
608 West Allegan, 3rd Floor
P.O. Box 30008
Lansing, MI 48909
www.michigan.gov/mde

Minnesota

State Department of Education
Personnel Licensing
610 Capitol Square Building
550 Cedar Street
St. Paul, MN 55101-2273
http://education.state.mn.us/mde/teacher_support

Mississippi

State Department of Education
Office of Educator Licensure
Central High School
359 North West Street
P.O. Box 771
Jackson, MS 39205-0771
www.mde.k12.ms.us/ed_licensure

Missouri

Department of Elementary and Secondary Education
Educator Certification
205 Jefferson Street
P.O. Box 480
Jefferson City, MO 65102-0480
www.dese.mo.gov/divteachqual/teachcert

Montana

Office of Public Instruction
Educator Licensure
1227 Eleventh Avenue East, Room 210
P.O. Box 202501
Helena, MT 59620-2501
www.opi.state.mt.us

Nebraska

State Department of Education
Teacher Education and Certification
301 Centennial Mall South
P.O. Box 94987
Lincoln, NE 68509-4987
www.nde.state.ne.us/tcert/tcmain.html

Nevada

State Department of Education
State Mail Room
1850 East Sahara, Suite 205
Las Vegas, NV 89104
www.doe.nv.gov/licensing.html

State Department of Education
Licensure Division
700 East Fifth Street
Carson City, NV 89701
www.doe.nv.gov/licensing.html

New Hampshire

State Department of Education
Bureau of Credentialing
101 Pleasant Street
Concord, NH 03301-3860
www.ed.state.nh.us/education/doe/organization/programsupport/
boc.htm

New Jersey

State Department of Education
Office of Professional Development and Licensing
Riverview Executive Plaza, Building 100, Room 29
P.O. Box 500
Trenton, NJ 08625-0503
www.nj.gov/njded/educators/license

New Mexico

New Mexico Public Education Department
Professional Licensure Unit
300 Don Gaspar
Santa Fe, NM 87501-2786
www.sde.state.nm.us/div/ais/lic

New York

State Education Department
Certification Unit
5N Education Building
Albany, NY 12234
www.nysed.gov/tcert

University of the State of New York
State Education Department
Teacher Certification and Licensing
89 Washington Avenue
Albany, NY 12234
http://usny.nysed.gov/licensing/teachercertlic.html

North Carolina

State Department of Public Instruction
Licensure Section
301 North Wilmington Street
Raleigh, NC 27601-2825
www.dpi.state.nc.us

North Dakota

State Department of Public Instruction
Education Standards and Practices Board
600 East Boulevard Avenue, Department 201
Bismarck, ND 58505-0440
www.dpi.state.nd.us

Ohio

State Department of Education
Office of Certification and Licensure
25 South Front Street, Mail Stop 105
Columbus, OH 43215-4183
www.ode.state.oh.us/teaching-profession/
    teacher/certification_licensure

Oklahoma

Oklahoma Commission for Teacher Preparation
4545 North Lincoln Boulevard, Suite 275
Oklahoma City, OK 73105-3418
www.octp.org/octp

State Department of Education
Professional Standards Section
2500 North Lincoln Boulevard Avenue, #212
Oklahoma City, OK 73105-4599
www.sde.state.ok.us/pro/tcert/profstd.html

Oregon

Teacher Standards and Practices Commission
465 Commercial Street Northeast
Salem, OR 97301
www.tspc.state.or.us

Pennsylvania

State Department of Education
Bureau of Teacher Certification and Preparation
333 Market Street
Harrisburg, PA 17126-0333
www.teaching.state.pa.us/teaching/site

Rhode Island

State Department of Education
Office of Teacher Preparation, Certification, & Professional
    Development
255 Westminster Street
Providence, RI 02903
www.ridoe.net/certification_pd

South Carolina

State Department of Education
Division of Educator Quality and Leadership
Landmark II Office Building
3700 Forest Drive, Suite 500
Columbia, SC 29204
www.scteachers.org

South Dakota

State Department of Education
Office of Accreditation and Teacher Quality
700 Governors Drive
Pierre, SD 57501-2291
http://doe.sd.gov/oatq/teachercert

Tennessee

State Department of Education
Office of Teacher Licensing
Andrew Johnson Tower, 4th Floor
710 James Robertson Parkway
Nashville, TN 37243-0377
www.state.tn.us/education/lic

Texas

Texas State Board for Educator Certification
1701 North Congress Avenue
Austin, TX 78701-1494
www.sbec.state.tx.us/sbeconline

Utah

Utah State Office of Education
Educator Licensing
250 East 500 South Street
P.O. Box 144200
Salt Lake City, UT 84114-4200
www.usoe.k12.ut.us/cert

Vermont

State Department of Education
Educator Licensing
120 State Street
Montpelier, VT 05620-2501
www.state.vt.us/educ/new/html/maincert.html

Virginia

State Department of Education
Division of Teacher Education and Licensure
P.O. Box 2120
Richmond, VA 23218-2120
www.pen.k12.va.us/VDOE/newvdoe/teached.html

Washington

Office of Superintendent of Public Instruction
Professional Education & Certification
Old Capitol Building
P.O. Box 4700
Olympia, WA 98504-7200
www.k12.wa.us/certification

West Virginia

State Department of Education

Teacher Certification

1900 Kanawha Boulevard East

Charleston, WV 25305

http://wvde.state.wv.us/certification

Wisconsin

State Superintendent of Public Instruction

Teacher Education, Professional Development, & Licensing

125 South Webster Street

P.O. Box 7841

Madison, WI 53707-7841

http://dpi.wi.gov/tepdl

Wyoming

State Department of Education

Professional Teaching Standards Board

Hathaway Building, 2nd Floor

2300 Capitol Avenue

Cheyenne, WY 82002-0050

http://ptsb.state.wy.us

State Child Care Licensing Agencies

CHECK ALSO WITH your local resource and referral agencies and county children's services. In many states, the family child care licensing is handled by each respective county. You may get information through your local county social services or county welfare department.

Alabama

Department of Human Resources
Child Care Services Division
Gordon Persons Bldg.
50 N. Ripley St.
Montgomery, AL 36130
www.dhr.state.al.us/page.asp?pageid=255

Alaska

Department of Health and Social Services
Division of Public Assistance
Child Care Program Office
619 E. Ship Creek Ave., Ste. 230
Anchorage, AK 99501-2341
http://health.hss.state.ak.us/dpa/programs/ccare

Arizona

Arizona Department of Health Services
Department of Licensure
150 N. 18th Ave., Ste. 400
Phoenix, AZ 85007
www.azdhs.gov/als/childcare

Arkansas

Department of Human Services
Division of Child Care and Early Childhood Education
Child Care Licensing Unit
700 Main St.
P.O. Box 1437, Slot 720
Little Rock, AR 72203-1437
www.state.ar.us/childcare

California

Department of Social Services
Community Care Licensing Division
Child Care Program
744 P St.
Sacramento, CA 95814
www.ccld.ca.gov

Colorado

Department of Human Services
Division of Child Care
1575 Sherman St., 1st Fl.
Denver, CO 80203-1714
www.cdhs.state.co.us/childcare/licensing.htm

Connecticut

CT Department of Public Health
Child Day Care Licensing
410 Capitol Ave.
Mail Station 12 DAC
P.O. Box 340308
Hartford, CT 06134-0308
www.dph.state.ct.us/brs/day_care/day_care.htm

Delaware

Department of Children, Youth, and Their Families
Office of Child Care Licensing
1825 Faulkland Rd.
Wilmington, DE 19805-1121
www.state.de.us/kids/occl.htm

District of Columbia

District of Columbia Health Regulation Administration
Child and Residential Care Facility Division
825 N. Capitol St. NE, 2nd Fl.
Washington, DC 20002
www.dchealth.dc.gov

Florida

Department of Children and Families
Child Care Regulation Office
1317 Winewood Blvd.
Bldg. 6, Rm. 389A
Tallahassee, FL 32399-0700
www.myflorida.com/childcare

Georgia

Bright from the Start:
Georgia Department of Early Care and Learning
10 Park Pl. South, Ste. 200
Atlanta, GA 30303
www.decal.state.ga.us

Hawaii

Department of Human Services
Benefit, Employment, and Support Services Division
820 Mililani St., Ste. 606
Honolulu, HI 96813-2936
www.state.hi.us/dhs

Idaho

Department of Health and Welfare
Bureau of Family and Community Services
450 W. State St.
Boise, ID 83720-0036
www.healthandwelfare.idaho.gov

Illinois

Department of Children and Family Services
Office of Licensing
406 E. Monroe St., Station 60
Springfield, IL 62701-1498
www.dhs.state.il.us/ts/childcaredevelopment/ccd

Indiana

Family and Social Services Administration
Division of Family and Children
Bureau of Child Development—Licensing Section
402 W. Washington St., Rm. W-386
Indianapolis, IN 46204
www.childcarefinder.in.gov

Iowa

Department of Human Services
Division of Behavioral Development and Protective Services
Child Care Unit
Hoover State Office Bldg., 5th Fl.
Des Moines, IA 50319-0114
www.dhs.state.ia.us/dhs2005/dhs_homepage/children_family/
    child_care

Kansas

Department of Health and Environment
Bureau of Child Care Licensing and Regulation
Curtis State Office Bldg.
1000 SW Jackson, Ste. 200
Topeka, KS 66612-1274
www.kdhe.state.ks.us/bcclr/child_care.html

Kentucky

Office of Inspector General
Division of Licensed Child Care
CHR Bldg.
275 E. Main St., 5E-A
Frankfort, KY 40621
http://chfs.ky.gov

Community Based Services
Division of Child Care
CHR Bldg.
275 E. Main St., 3C-F
Frankfort, KY 40621
http://chfs.ky.gov

Louisiana

Department of Social Services
Executive Office of the Secretary
Bureau of Licensing
2751 Wooddale
P.O. Box 3078
Baton Rouge, LA 70821
www.dss.state.la.us/departments/os/licensing_.html

Maine

Child Care Licensing
Maine Department of Health and Human Services
Marquardt Bldg.
11 State House Station, 221 State St.
Augusta, ME 04333-0011
www.state.me.us/dhs/occhs/cclicensing.htm

Maryland

Department of Human Resources
Child Care Administration
311 W. Saratoga St., 1st Fl.
Baltimore, MD 21201
www.dhr.state.md.us

Massachusetts

Office of Child Care Services
600 Washington St., 6th Fl., Ste. 6100
Boston, MA 02111
www.qualitychildcare.org

Michigan

Child Day Care Licensing
Family Independence Agency
Office of Children and Adult Licensing
P.O. Box 30037
Lansing, MI 48909-8150
www.michigan.gov/dhs

Minnesota

Department of Human Services
Division of Licensing
444 Lafayette Rd. North
St. Paul, MN 55155-3842
www.dhs.state.mn.us/licensing

Mississippi

Child Care Facilities Licensure
Mississippi State Department
570 E. Woodrow Wilson Dr.
Jackson, MS 39215-1700
www.msdh.state.ms.us

Missouri

Missouri Department of Social Services
Bureau of Child Care
221 W. High St.
P.O. Box 1527
Jefferson City, MO 65102-1527
www.dss.mo.gov/cd/childcare

Montana

Department of Public Health and Human Services
Quality Assurance Division
Licensing Bureau
Child Care Licensing Program
2401 Colonial Dr.
P.O. Box 202953
Helena, MT 59620-2953
www.dphhs.mt.gov/aboutus/divisions/qualityassurance

Nebraska

Department of Health and Human Services—Regulation and
    Licensure
Credentialing Division
Child Care Licensing Program
P.O. Box 94986
Lincoln, NE 68509-4986
www.hhs.state.ne.us/crl/childcare/childcareindex.htm

Nevada

Department of Human Resources
Division of Child and Family Services
Bureau of Services for Child Care
400 W. King St., Ste. 230
Carson City, NV 89703
www.dcfs.state.nv.us/page23.html

New Hampshire

Department of Health and Human Services
Office of Program Support
Bureau of Child Care Licensing
129 Pleasant St.
Concord, NH 03301-3857
www.dhhs.state.nh.us/dhhs/bccl

New Jersey

Department of Human Services
Office of Licensing
Quakerbridge Plaza, Bldg. 6
P.O. Box 717
Trenton, NJ 08625-0717
www.state.nj.us/humanservices/dyfs/licensing.html

New Mexico

Department of Children, Youth, and Families
Child Services Unit/Licensing
1920 5th St.
P.O. Box Drawer 5160
Santa Fe, NM 87502-5160
www.newmexicokids.org

New York

Office of Children and Family Services
Capital View Office Park
Bureau of Early Childhood Services
52 Washington St., Rm. 338, North Bldg.
Rensselaer, NY 12144-2796
www.dfa.state.ny.us

Department of Health and Mental Hygiene
Bureau of Day Care
2 Lafayette St., 22nd Fl.
New York, NY 10007
www.nyc.gov/html/doh/html/dc/dclh.shtml

North Carolina

Division of Child Development
Regulatory Services Section
319 Chapanoke Rd., Ste. 120
Raleigh, NC 27603
http://ncchildcare.dhhs.state.nc.us/providers/pv_sn2_lr.asp

North Dakota

Department of Human Services
Early Childhood Services
600 E. Blvd. Ave.
State Capital Bldg.
Bismarck, ND 58505-0250
www.ndchildcare.org

Ohio

Department of Job and Family Services
Bureau of Child Care and Development
30 E. Broad St., 32nd Fl.
Columbus, OH 43215-3414
http://jfs.ohio.gov/cdc

Oklahoma

Department of Human Services
Division of Child Care
P.O. Box 25352
Oklahoma City, OK 73125-0352
www.okdhs.org/childcare/providerinfo/provinfo_licensing.htm

Oregon

Department of Employment
Child Care Division
875 Union St. NE
Salem, OR 97311
http://findit.emp.state.or.us/childcare

Pennsylvania

Department of Public Welfare
Bureau of Child Day Care
Office of Children, Youth, and Families
Health and Welfare Bldg., Rm. 131
P.O. Box 2675
Harrisburg, PA 17105-2675
www.dpw.state.pa.us/child/childcare/003670906.htm

Puerto Rico

Department of Family
Licensing Office
P.O. Box 11398
Santurce, PR 00910
www.nncc.org/states/sjpr.html

Rhode Island

Department of Children, Youth, and Families
Day Care Licensing Unit
101 Friendship St.
Providence, RI 02903-3716
www.dcyf.state.ri.gov/licensing.htm

South Carolina

Department of Social Services
Division of Child Day Care Licensing and Regulatory Services
2638 Two Notch Rd., Ste. 200
Columbia, SC 29204
www.state.sc.us/dss/cdclrs

South Dakota

Department of Social Services
Child Care Services
Kneip Bldg.
700 Governors Dr.
Pierre, SD 57501-2291
www.state.sd.us/social/ccs/ccshome.htm

Tennessee

Department of Human Services
Child and Adult Care Services
Citizens Plaza Bldg., 15th Fl.
400 Deaderick St.
Nashville, TN 37248-0001
www.state.tn.us/humanserv/childcare.htm

Texas

Department of Family and Protective Services
Child Care Licensing
P.O. Box 149030
701 W. 51st St.
Austin, TX 78714-9030
www.dfps.state.tx.us/child_care/about_child_care_licensing

Utah

Department of Health
Office of Child Care Licensing
P.O. Box 142003
Salt Lake City, UT 84114-2003
www.health.utah.gov/licensing

Vermont

Department for Children and Families
Child Developmental Division
Child Care Licensing Unit
103 S. Main St., 2 North
Waterbury, VT 05676
www.dcf.state.vt.us/cdd

Virgin Islands

Department of Human Services
Division of Children, Youth, and Families
Child Care Licensing
Knud Hansen Complex, Bldg. A
1303 Hospital Ground
Charlotte Amalie, VI 00802
http://nrc.uchsc.edu/STATES/VI/virginislands.htm

Virginia

Department of Social Services
Division of Licensing Programs
7 N. 8th St.
Richmond, VA 23219
www.dss.state.va.us/division/license

Washington

Department of Social and Health Services
Economic Services Administration
Division of Child Care and Early Learning
P.O. Box 45480
Olympia, WA 98504-5480
www1.dshs.wa.gov/esa/dccel

West Virginia

Department of Health and Human Resources
Bureau for Children and Families
Office of Children and Family Policy
Division of Early Care and Education
350 Capitol St., Rm. 730
Charleston, WV 25301-3711
www.wvdhhr.org/bcf

Wisconsin

Division of Children and Family Services
Bureau for Regulation and Licensing
1 W. Wilson St., Rm. 534
P.O. Box 8916
Madison, WI 53708-8916
www.dhfs.state.wi.us/rl_dcfs

Wyoming

Department of Family Services
Division of Early Childhood
2300 Capitol Ave.
Hathaway Bldg., 3rd Fl.
Cheyenne, WY 82002-0490
http://dfsweb.state.wy.us

BIBLIOGRAPHY

Ayers, William. *The Good Preschool Teacher: Six Teachers Reflect on Their Lives.* New York: Teachers College Press, 1989.

Beaty, Janice J. *Skills for Preschool Teachers.* New York: Merrill, 1992.

Berrick, Jill Duerr. "Welfare and Child Care: The Intricacies of Competing Social Values." *Social Work* 36 (July 1991): 345.

Bureau of Labor Statistics, U.S. Department of Labor. *Occupational Outlook Handbook*, 2004–5 ed. www.bls.gov/oco.

Cahan, Emily D. *Past Caring: A History of U.S. Preschool Care and Education for the Poor, 1820–1965.* New York: National Center for Children in Poverty, 1989.

Celis, William, III. "Governors Announce Plan to Help Preschool Children." *New York Times* (August 2, 1992): 12.

Celis, William, III. "Study Suggests Head Start Helps Beyond School." *New York Times* (April 20, 1993): A9.

Celis, William, III. "Study Urges a Preschool Role for Businesses." *New York Times* (March 1, 1991): A14.

Center for the Childcare Workforce, A Project of the American Federation of Teachers Educational Foundation. "Current Data on the Salaries and Benefits of the U.S. Early Childhood Education Workforce," 2004. www.ccw.org/pubs/2004 compendium.pdf.

Chadwick, Bruce, and Tim B. Heaton. *Statistical Handbook on the American Family*. Phoenix, Ariz.: Oryx Press, 1990.

Cherry, Clare. *Family Day Care Providers Management Guide*. Redding, Calif.: Fearon Teacher Aids, 1991.

Child Care Employee Project. *Who Cares? Child Care Teachers and the Quality of Care in America: Report of the National Child Care Staffing Study*. Pamphlet. Oakland, Calif.: Child Care Employee Project, 1989.

Children's Defense Fund. *The State of America's Children*. Washington, DC: The Fund, 1991.

Children's Defense Fund. *The State of America's Children*. Washington, DC: The Fund, 2004. www.cdfwebstore.com/ online/scstore/Greenbook2004.pdf.

Chira, Susan. "Report Says Too Many Aren't Ready for School." *New York Times* (December 8, 1991): 18.

Cohen, Julie A. "On-Site Childcare: Two Solutions." *Personnel* 67 (November 1990): 1.

Cole, Kevin N. "Effects of Preschool Integration for Children with Disabilities." *Exceptional Children* 58 (September 1991): 36.

Cook, Ruth E. *Adapting Early Childhood Curricula for Children with Special Needs*. New York: Merrill, 1992.

Cronin, Michael P. "Taking Care of Sick Kids." *Inc.* 15 (August 1993): 27.

Cyert Center for Early Education at Carnegie Mellon University. "The Reggio Emilia Approach," 2004. Pittsburgh, Pa. www.cmu.edu/cyert-center/rea.htm.

Danish, William J. "Dependent Care: The Invisible Benefit." *HR Focus* 69 (March 1992): 8.

Davidson, Jane Ilene. *Children and Computers Together in the Early Childhood Classroom.* Albany, N.Y.: Delmar Publishers, 1989.

Decker, Celia Anita. *Planning and Administering Early Childhood Programs.* New York: Merrill, 1992.

Devries, Rheta. *Constructivist Early Education: Overview and Comparison with Other Programs.* Washington, DC: National Association for the Education of Young Children, 1990.

Dodge, Diane Trister. *A Trainer's Guide to Caring for Preschool Children: A Supervised, Self-Instructional Training Program.* Washington, DC: Teaching Strategies, 1990.

Dumas, Lynne S. "Best Places for Preschoolers." *Working Mother* 16 (July 1993): 48.

Edwards, Linda Carol. *Affective Development and the Creative Arts: A Process Approach to Early Childhood Education.* Columbus: Merrill Publishing Co., 1990.

Employment Policy Foundation. *The American Workplace 2005: The Changing Nature of Employee Benefits.* Washington, DC, 2005. www.epf.org/pubs/labordayreports/2005/AWR2005 ExecSummary.pdf.

Essa, Eva. *An Early Childhood Curriculum: From Developmental Model to Application.* Albany, N.Y.: Delmar Publishers, 1992.

Federal Interagency Forum on Child and Family Statistics. *America's Children: Key National Indicators of Well-Being,* 2005. Washington, DC: U.S. Government Printing Office. http://childstats.ed.gov/pubs.asp.

Fernandez, John P. *The Politics and Reality of Family Care in Corporate America*. Lanham, Md.: Lexington Books, 1990.

Gharavi, Gloria Junkin. "Music Skills for Preschool Teachers: Needs and Solutions." *Arts Education Policy Review* 94 (January–February 1993): 27.

Gibson, Virginia. "Seeking Solutions to Work/Family Dilemmas." *HR Focus* 68 (December 1991): 24.

Herr, Judy. "Childcare Providers and Parents: Let's Work Together for America's Young Children." *Personnel* 68 (September 1991): 15.

Herr, Judith. *Creative Resources for the Early Childhood Classroom*. Albany, N.Y.: Delmar Publishers, 1990.

Hinds, Michael deCourcy. "Nationwide Revolution in Education Is Giving Handicapped a Headstart." *New York Times* (July 17, 1991): A19, B7.

Horn, Wade F. "Head Start: Facing New Challenges." *Children Today* 19 (May–June 1990): 4.

Hymes, James L. *Early Childhood Education: 20 Years in Review (1971–1990)*. Washington, DC: National Association for the Education of Young Children, 1991.

International Nanny Association. "So You Want to Be a Nanny . . . Answers to Questions People Often Ask About In-Home Child Care," 2002. www.nanny.org/sywtban.htm.

Joesch, Jutta A. "The Effect of the Price of Child Care on AFDC Mothers' Paid Work Behavior." *Family Relations* 40 (April 1991): 161.

Kagan, Sharon Lynn. *Excellence in Early Childhood Education: Defining Characteristics and Next-Decade Strategies*. Washington, DC: U.S. Government Printing Office, 1990.

Kisker, Ellen Eliason. *A Profile of Child Care Settings: Early Education and Care in 1990.* Washington, DC: U.S. Department of Education, 1991.

Lawton, Kim A. "Adventures in Federal Babysitting: As Congress Moves Ahead with Childcare Legislation, Religious Groups Argue About the Implications for Church-Based Centers." *Christianity Today* 34 (May 14, 1990): 34.

Luxenburg, Stan. "All Work and No Playtime." *Scholastic Update* 124 (September 6, 1991): 12.

Marhoefer, Patricia E. *Caring for the Developing Child.* Albany, N.Y.: Delmar Publishers, 1992.

Miller, Janice J. "Dependent Care and the Workplace: An Analysis of Management and Employee Perceptions." *Journal of Business Ethics* 10 (November 1991): 863.

Minnesota Department of Education. *A Report to the Minnesota Legislature on the Way to Grow/School Readiness Program.* St. Paul: Minnesota Department of Education, 1993.

Murphy, Clennie H. Jr. "Head Start at 25." *Children Today* (May–June 1990).

National Association of Child Care Resource and Referral Agencies. "Child Care in America Fact Sheet." http://nccrra .net/docs/Child_Care_In_America_Facts.pdf.

National Association for the Education of Young Children. "Associate Degree Program Accreditation." November 15, 2005. www.naeyc.org.

Noble, Barbara Presley. "A Corporate Collaboration for Care: Companies Create a $25.4 Million Initiative for Their Employees' Dependent Care Needs." *New York Times* (September 27, 1992): F27.

O'Connell, Martin. *Who's Minding the Kids?: Child Care Arrangements.* Washington, DC: U.S. Government Printing Office, 1992.

Osborn, D. Keith. *Early Childhood Education in Historical Perspective.* Athens, Ga.: Daye Press, 1991.

Paasche, Carol. *Children with Special Needs in Early Childhood Setting: Identification, Intervention, Mainstreaming.* Menlo Park, Calif.: Addison-Wesley, 1990.

Reynolds, Larry. "Advocates Target Childcare After Leave Bill Passes." *HR Focus* 70 (May 1993): 1.

Ritter, Anne. "Dependent Care Proves Profitable." *Personnel* 67 (March 1990): 12.

Schiller, Pamela Byrne. *Managing Quality Child Care Centers: A Comprehensive Manual for Administrators.* New York: Teachers College Press, 1990.

Sciarra, Dorothy June. *Developing and Administering a Child Care Center.* Albany, N.Y.: Delmar Publishers, 1990.

Shaman, Diana. "For Company Day Care, Naptime's Over: Centers Growing, Helping to Recruit and Retain Staffs." *New York Times* (March 28, 1993): R9.

Shellenbarger, Sue. "Firms Fund Changes Independent Care." *Wall St. Journal* (December 30, 1992): B1.

Smith, Bob. "On the Outside Looking In: What Parents Want from Childcare." *Personnel* 68 (September 1991): 14.

Solomon, Stephen D. "Check Your Dependent Care Policy." *Inc.* 11 (December 1989): 143.

Spragins, Ellyn E. "Changed Lives: The Effects of the Perry Preschool Program on Youths Through Age 19." *Study.* Ypsilanti, Mich.: High/Scope Press, 1984.

Spragins, Ellyn E. "Low-Cost Child Care." *Inc.* 15 (March 1993): 34.

Taylor, Barbara J. *A Child Goes Forth: A Curriculum Guide for Preschool Children.* New York: Macmillan, 1991.

Tepperman, Jean, and Jessine Foss. "Unions in Child Care?" *Children's Advocate* (May–June 2004). *Action Alliance for Children.* Oakland, Calif.: www.4children.org/news/504 union.htm.

United States Census Bureau. "Ranking of Percent of Children under 6 Years Old with All Parents in the Labor Force." 2004 American Community Survey. http://factfinder.census.gov/ servlet/GRTTable.

United States Congress. *Act for Better Child Care Services of 1989.* Washington, DC: U.S. Government Printing Office, 1989.

United States Congress. *The Economic and Social Benefits of Early Childhood Education: Hearing Before the Subcommittee on Education and Health of the Joint Economic Committee.* Washington, DC: U.S. Government Printing Office, 1989.

United States Congress. *Family and Medical Leave Act of 1993: Report Together with Minority and Additional Views.* Washington, DC: U.S. Government Printing Office, 1993.

United States Congress. *The Future of Head Start: Hearing before the Subcommittee on Education and Health of the Joint Economic Committee.* Washington, DC: U.S. Government Printing Office, 1990.

United States Congress. *Head Start: A Child Development Program 25 Years . . . Building America's Future 1965–1990.* Washington, DC: U.S. Government Printing Office, 1990.

United States Congress. *Smart Start: The Community Collaborative for Early Childhood Development Act of 1989*. Washington, DC: U.S. Government Printing Office, 1989.

United States Department of Education. Introduction: No Child Left Behind, "Four Pillars of NCLB." Washington, DC. www.ed.gov/print/nclb/overview/intro.

United States Department of Education. "A Profile of Child Care Settings: Early Education and Care in 1991." Washington, DC: U.S. Department of Education, 1991.

United States Department of Labor. "Women in the Labor Force: A Databook." Washington, DC: U.S. Department of Labor, May 2005. www.bls.gov/cps/wlf-databook-2005.pdf

United States Department of Labor, Women's Bureau. *Facts on Working Women*, No. 89-3. Washington, DC: U.S. Government Printing Office, 1989.

United States Department of Labor, Women's Bureau. "Work and Family Resource Kit: Dependent Care Options." Washington, DC: U.S. Department of Labor, 1992.

United States Department of Labor, Women's Bureau. "Working Mothers and Their Children." *Facts on Working Women*, No. 89-3. Washington, DC: U.S. Government Printing Office, 1989.

United States Department of Labor Statistics. *Occupational Outlook Handbook*, 1992–93 ed. Indianapolis, Ind.: JIST Works, Inc., 1992.

Wash, Darrel Patrick. "Child Day Care Services: An Industry at a Crossroads." *Monthly Labor Review* 113 (December 1990): 17.

Weiser, Margaret G. *Infant/Toddler Care and Education*. New York: Merrill, 1991.

The White House. Executive Summary: "Good Start, Grow
    Smart: The Bush Administration's Early Childhood
    Initiative." Washington, DC. www.whitehouse.gov/infocus/
    earlychildhood/sect1.html.
Whitebook, Marcy. *Working for Quality Child Care*. Berkeley,
    Calif.: Child Care Employee Project, 1989.
Williams, Leslie R., and Doris Pronin Fromberg, eds. *Encyclopedia
    of Early Childhood Education*. New York: Garland Publishing
    Inc., 1992.
Williams, Monte. "Oh Baby: On-Site Childcare Coming Out of
    the Dark Ages." *Advertising Age* 62 (February 25, 1991): 24.
Wines, Michael. "Bush Urges Head Start Increase, and Debate on
    Its Impact Follows." *New York Times* (January 22, 1992): A12.
Wison, Lavisa Cam. *Infants & Toddlers: Curriculum and Teaching*.
    Albany, N.Y.: Delmar Publishers, 1990.
Wolf, Douglas A. "Child-Care Use Among Welfare Mothers: A
    Dynamic Analysis." *Journal of Family Issues* 12 (December
    1991): 519.
Working for America Institute. "Union Presidents Speak Out on
    Child Care." *Connections*, Volume 2, Number 1 (June 2003).
    www.workingforamerica.org/documents/connections_files/0
    62003c2.htm.
Zigler, Edward. "Head Start Falls Behind." *New York Times* (June
    27, 1992): 15.

About the Author

Renee Wittenberg is a child care specialist, writer, and proud mother of two grown children. She graduated from Bemidji State University (Minnesota) with a Bachelor of Science degree in social work with emphasis on early childhood psychology and development. She has also earned a Master of Science degree in education from Saint Cloud State University (Minnesota). She currently works as an instructional designer.

Wittenberg is the author of articles on child care, child care providers, and the need for quality child care programs. She has also published articles in *First Teacher* magazine on the subjects of preschool children's development and preschool activities. She has operated her own home business as a licensed group child care provider and founded a local child care providers association. Wittenberg also has worked with child care services for the State of Minnesota Employment Services Department.